EAST MEETS WEST

CHINESE ESL STUDENTS IN NORTH AMERICAN HIGHER EDUCATION

EDUCATION IN A COMPETITIVE AND GLOBALIZING WORLD

Additional books in this series can be found on Nova's website under the Series tab.

Additional e-books in this series can be found on Nova's website under the e-book tab.

EAST MEETS WEST

CHINESE ESL STUDENTS IN NORTH AMERICAN HIGHER EDUCATION

JINYAN HUANG

EDITOR

nova publishers
New York

For permission to use material from this book please contact us:
Telephone 631-231-7269; Fax 631-231-8175
Web Site: http://www.novapublishers.com

NOTICE TO THE READER

Library of Congress Cataloging-in-Publication Data

ISBN: 978-1-62618-195-3

Published by Nova Science Publishers, Inc. † New York

To my lovely children Joy, Jerry, Jayden, and Jade

CONTENTS

List of Tables   ix

List of Figures   xi

Preface   xiii

About the Editor   xix

PART 1: CHINESE ESL STUDENTS   1

Chapter 1   Understanding Chinese ESL Students' Learning Approaches   3
               Jinyan Huang and Peter Cowden

Chapter 2   Understanding Chinese ESL Students' Academic Anxiety   15
               Jinyan Huang and Shuangli Su

Chapter 3   Confidence Levels of Chinese ESL Students' English Abilities   27
               Jinyan Huang and Shuangli Su

Chapter 4   Chinese ESL Students' Learning Challenges and Coping Strategies   35
               Jinyan Huang and Don Klinger

PART 2: EAST MEETS WEST   47

Chapter 5   The Factors Affecting Chinese ESL Students' Academic Learning   49
               Jinyan Huang and Vince Rinaldo

Chapter 6   The Impact of Cultural Differences on Chinese ESL Students'
               Academic Learning   63
               Jinyan Huang and Kathleen Brown

Chapter 7   The Impact of Academic Skills on Chinese ESL Students'
               Academic Listening   75
               Jinyan Huang and Shuangli Su

Chapter 8   The Merging of Two Cultures in the Classroom   83
               Jinyan Huang and Shuangli Su

PART 3: WEST MEETS EAST   **93**

Chapter 9   North American Professors' Use of English Affects Chinese
                   ESL Students' Academic Listening   **95**
                   Jinyan Huang and Shuangli Su

Chapter 10   North American Professors' Teaching Styles Affect Chinese
                   ESL Students' Academic Listening   **107**
                   Jinyan Huang and Shuangli Su

Chapter 11   The Factors Impacting North Amercian Professors' Evaluation
                   of Chinese ESL Students' Academic Writing   **125**
                   Jinyan Huang and Chandra Foote

Chapter 12   North American Professors' Social Support
                   Facilitates Chinese ESL Students' Academic Learning   **141**
                   R. Michael Smith and Ling Zhou

Index   **149**

LIST OF TABLES

Table 3.1.	Result of Demographic Information	28
Table 3.2.	CESL Students' Responses and Percents Selecting Each Scale Point	29
Table 3.3.	CESL Students' Reported Confidence in English Abilities for Academic Listening	30
Table 3.4.	Percentage of Class Lecture CESL Students Comprehend	33
Table 7.3.	Suggestions for CESL Students	80
Table 10.1.	American Instructional Factors Affecting CESL Students' Academic Listening	114
Table 11.1.	Descriptive Statistics	132
Table 11.2.	Paired Samples t-Tests Results	132
Table 11.3.	Variance Components for a Random Effects p x l x r G-Study Design	133
Table 11.4.	Variance Components for Random Effects p x r G-Study Designs	134
Table 11.5.	Summary of G-coefficients	135
Appendix B.	Holistic Rating Rubric (6-point scale; half point allowed)	137

LIST OF FIGURES

Figure 5.1.   A System of Factors Affecting CESL Students' Academic Learning   **51**

PREFACE

The number of English-as-a-second-language (ESL) students has more than doubled since the 1980s and has recently grown significantly at North American universities; Chinese ESL (CESL) students from the People's Republic of China (PRC) represent the single largest group of ESL students (Canadian Bureau for International Education, 2009; Institute of International Education, 2010). These CESL students have generally received their K-12 education and many of them have received their undergraduate degrees in PRC. The academic learning experience of this group of CESL graduate students has important educational implications for university administrators and educators (Huang and Klinger, 2006; Huang and Rinaldo, 2009).

CESL students are from a very different educational system and cultural background. Previous research has indicated that there are considerable challenges faced by CESL students in their academic studies at North American universities, e.g., their unfamiliarity with North American culture, their inadequate English proficiency, their social and emotional challenges, their financial difficulties, etc. (Chen, 1999; Huang and Brown, 2009; Huang, 2004, 2005, 2009; Huang and Klinger, 2006; Lin, 2002; Liu, 1994; Myles, Qian and Cheng, 2002; Wan, 2001; Zhong, 1996). For example, Chinese culture is very different from the culture of North America and the cultural differences have a negative impact on their academic studies (Huang and Brown, 2009; Huang and Rinaldo, 2009). This is because students from different cultures learn in different ways, and may differ in their learning styles, self-expressions and communication styles (Bennett, 1999).

All these challenges may negatively affect the academic study of these CESL students (e.g., Feng, 1991; Huang, 1998; Huang, 2004, 2005; Sun and Chen, 1997; Upton, 1989). For example, these challenges may contribute to academic anxiety for CESL students; and consequently academic anxiety negatively affects their academic learning at North American universities (Feng, 1991; Huang, 1998; Sun and Chen, 1997; Upton, 1989). However, given their generally high rate of success in academic studies and contributions to North American society (Johnson, 2001), these students do develop effective coping strategies to meet these challenges (Lin, 2002). Further, North American professors might have helped or may help CESL students overcome their challenges so that they could achieve academic success.

The purpose of this book, therefore, is three-fold: a) to understand CESL students' learning approaches, academic anxiety, confidence levels of English skills, and learning challenges and coping strategies; b) to explore the impact of various factors (e.g., cultural differences) on their academic learning; and c) to examine the effects of North American professors' teaching and assessment practices as well as their social support on CESL students' academic learning at North American universities. Accordingly, this book, which is a collection of empirical studies and articles, contains three parts and each part contains four chapters. Each chapter presents a main theme.

The first chapter explores CESL students' academic learning through cultural studies perspectives by examining the concept of identity; cultural and linguistic context; CESL students as quiet and passive learners; different classroom teaching methods experienced in both cultures; surface learners vs. deep learners; different culture worlds; and the concept of *social* communicative competence. The purpose of this chapter is to gain a better understanding of CESL students' challenges as well as their learning approaches at North American universities. It is argued that quiet, passive and surface learners are perhaps incorrect descriptors of CESL students who are studying at North American universities.

The second chapter presents a qualitative study which examined whether or not four CESL Ph.D. students were experiencing high levels of academic anxiety at two North American universities and if so, their perceptions of the factors contributing to their academic anxiety, the impact of academic anxiety on their learning, and their strategies for coping with academic anxiety. The results show that two participants were experiencing high levels of academic anxiety. Majors that involve more language usage, such as education, political studies, and religious studies, seem to cause greater levels of academic anxiety than those majors that rely more on graphs, tables, numbers and symbols, such as mathematics, biology, and chemistry. The major sources of high levels of academic anxiety, as reported by these two participants, are financial difficulties, language barriers, cultural differences, being away from family and friends, and difficulty in finding employment. Academic anxiety decreases their self-confidence and also has a negative impact on their academic learning, social life, and personal feelings.

The third chapter reports a proportion of a study that investigates their English academic listening challenges as reported by seventy-eight CESL students at an American university. Specifically, this chapter focuses on CESL students' reported confidence in their English abilities for academic listening. Their self-ratings show that reading ability and grammar are the strongest areas, and listening and speaking are the weakest areas. Ninety-two percent of the participants reported having difficulties in understanding English academic lectures. Arts students who had been studying at this American university for less than one year reported that they could only understand sixty to seventy percent of the lectures in their majors.

The fourth chapter presents a qualitative study that investigated four CESL graduate students' perceptions of the challenges they face and the coping strategies they implemented in their English academic learning at two North American universities. They reported experiencing the following seven major challenges in their academic learning: a) financial difficulties; b) problems in using English for academic purposes; c) frustrations in becoming a permanent resident; d) difficulty in adapting to the classroom learning environment; e) lack of critical thinking skills; f) acculturation problems; and g) loneliness and academic anxiety. For each of the seven challenges they have developed corresponding coping strategies.

The fifth chapter reports the results of an empirical study that investigated four CESL graduate students' perceptions of the factors contributing to or impeding their English academic learning at two North American universities. They reported that the following six major factors affect their academic learning: a) socio-cultural factors, b) educational factors, c) linguistic factors, d) cognitive factors, e) affective factors, and f) financial factors. Their satisfaction with and concerns about their academic learning at these two universities were also examined.

When Confucianism meets Constructivism in North American universities, our classrooms are failing to meet the educational expectations of CESL students. The sixth chapter discusses the cultural differences that affect CESL students' academic learning at North American universities. Specifically, CESL students mentioned six areas where they feel discomfort: a) they feel uncomfortable with the classroom behavior of North American students; b) they question the value of a professorial focus on discussion rather than lecture; c) they query the professor's failure to follow the textbook; d) they feel there is too much emphasis on group work; e) they note a lack of lecture summaries along with an apparent lack of organization; f) they share no common interests (e.g. sports, religion) with their North American counterparts. This chapter also provides implications for North American professors.

The seventh chapter presents a proportion of a study that examined CESL students' challenges in understanding academic lectures at an American university. It focuses on the effects of the following academic skills on CESL students' lecture comprehension: a) text previewing, b) note-taking, c) short-term memory, and d) English language skills. This chapter also offers suggestions for CESL students about how to improve their academic skills for English lecture comprehension at American universities.

The eighth chapter presents an empirical study that investigated four CESL graduate students' perceptions of the major differences between North American and Chinese classroom teaching styles. Major differences in the following five areas were identified: a) the teacher's role, b) the student's role, c) the form of class organization, d) the teacher's expectations, and e) the student's expectations. It then explored these four CESL graduate students' North American classroom learning reality. Finally, the study examined how they adjusted their classroom learning strategies and approaches accordingly so that they could adapt to the North American classroom environment.

The ninth chapter examines how American professors' use of English in class affects CESL students' understanding of academic lectures. The results show that a) the rapidness of professors' English speech; b) professors' lack of clear pronunciation; c) professors' use of long and complex sentences; d) professors' use of colloquial and slang expressions; e) professors' lack of clear definition of terms and concepts; and f) professors' use of discourse markers affect CESL students' English academic listening at an American university. It offers important suggestions for American professors as how to make their lectures more accessible to CESL students.

The tenth chapter examines the impact of American classroom instructional factors on CESL students' English academic listening. They reported that the following instructional factors affected their English academic listening at an American university: a) lecture organization, b) use of textbooks, c) blackboard writing, d) lecture summary, e) amount of student participation, and f) amount of group work. The chapter also offers suggestions for American professors about how to make their lectures more accessible to CESL students.

The eleventh chapter presents a quantitative study that examined how CESL graduate students' academic writing tasks were evaluated by their American professors. Specifically, this study examined score variations and differences in the reliability of ratings between CESL - and Native English (NE-) authored papers in a graduate course at an American university. Generalizability (*G*-) theory was used as a framework for analysis because it is powerful in detecting rater variability and the relative contributions of multiple sources of error. The results indicate that CESL papers received consistently lower scores than NE papers. The *G*-coefficients for CESL and NE papers were considerably different revealing concern about the reliability of ratings of CESL papers. The significant increase in the number of CESL students pursuing graduate degrees in North American institutions warrants further research to determine the extent to which consistency differences affect the validity of the assessment of CESL students' writing and to identify ways to alleviate these differences.

The twelfth chapter presents a case study that examined how an American professor's social support facilitates a CESL graduate student's academic learning at an American university. This chapter is a case study based on the first-year experiences of a two-year longitudinal study. It describes how a North American professor provided an extended social support system for a CESL student in an effort to facilitate the student's academic learning. Focusing on Maslow's hierarchy of needs as the conceptual framework, the study describes how each of the student's needs: physiological; safety; love and belongingness; self-esteem; and self-actualization were met to facilitate the learning process and academic success of the CESL student.

This book provides substantial and detailed information on CESL students about their educational and cultural backgrounds, learning approaches, and learning challenges and coping strategies. Further, it thoroughly investigates the factors that impact their academic learning at North American universities. Finally, it empirically examines the effects of North American professors' teaching and assessment practices as well as their social support on CESL students' academic learning at North American universities. In addition, this book has offered important implications for CESL students and their North American professors as well as expanding our understanding of cross-cultural learning issues in the context of ESL education at North American universities.

REFERENCES

Bennett, S. (1999). *Comprehensive multicultural education: Theory and practice.* Allyn and Bacon, Boston, MA

Canadian Bureau for International Education. (2009). Retrieved October 28, 2009 from the World Wide Web: *http://www.cbie.ca*

Chen, C. P. (1999). Common stressors among international college students: Research and counseling implications. *Journal of College Conseling, 2,* 49-65.

Feng, J. H. (1991). *The adaptation of Students from the People's Republic of China to an American Academic Culture.* Reports (ERIC Document Reproduction Service No. ED 329 833).

Institute of International Education. (2010). *Open Doors Online.* Retrieved July 21, 2010 from the World Wide Web: *http://www.opendoors.iienetwork.org.*

Huang, J. (2005). Challenges of academic listening in English: Reports by Chinese students. *College Student Journal, 39*(3), 553-569.

Huang, J. (2004). Voices from Chinese students: Professors' use of English affects academic listening. *College Student Journal, 38*(2), 212-223.

Huang, J. (2005). Challenges of academic listening in English: Reports by Chinese students. *College Student Journal, 39*(3), 553-569.

Huang, J. (2009). What happens when two cultures meet in the classroom? *Journal of Instructional Psychology, 36*(4), 335-342.

Huang, J. (1998). *Students' learning difficulties in a second language speaking classroom.* Paper presented at the Annual Meeting of the American Educational Research Association, San Diego, CA. (ERIC Document Reproduction Service No. ED 420193)

Huang, J., and Brown, K. (2009). Cultural factors affecting Chinese ESL students' academic learning. *Education, 129*(4), 643-653.

Huang, J., and Klinger, D. (2006). Chinese graduate students at North American universities: Learning challenges and coping strategies. *The Canadian and International Education Journal, 35*(2), 48-61.

Huang, J., and Rinaldo, V. (2009). Factors affecting Chinese graduate students' cross-cultural learning at North American universities. *International Journal of Applied Educational Studies, 4*(1), 1-13.

Johnson, J. M. (2001). *Human resources contributions to US science and engineering from China.* SRS Issue Brief. (ERIC Document Reproduction Service No. ED 449026)

Lin. L. (2002). *The learning experiences of Chinese graduate students in American social science programs.* Paper presented at the Annual Conference of the Comparative and International Education Society. Orlando, FL.

Liu, D. L. (1994). *Deep sociocultural transfer and its effect on second language speakers' communication.* Paper presented at the annual meeting of the Teachers of English to Speakers of Other Languages, Baltimore, MD.

Myles, J., Quian, J., and Chen , L. (2002). International and new immigrant students' adaptations to the social and cultural life at a Canadian university. *Connections and Complexities: The Internationalization of Canadian Higher Education,* Occasional Papers in Higher Education, Vol. 11, Winnipeg, Center for Research and Development in Higher Education.

Sun, W., and Chen, G. M. (1997). *Dimensions of difficulties Mainland Chinese students encounter in the United States.* Paper presented at the 6th International Conference in Cross-Cultural Communication, Tempe, AZ. (ERIC Document Reproduction Service No. ED 408635)

Upton, T. A. (1989). Chinese students, American universities, and cultural confrontation. *MinneTESOL Journal, 7*, 9-28.

Wan, G. F. (2001). The learning experience of Chinese students in American universities: A cross-cultural perspective. *College Student Journal, 35*, 28-44.

Zhong, M. (1996). *Chinese students and scholars in the US: An intercultural adaptation process.* Paper presented at the 82nd Annual Meeting of the Speech Communication Association, San Diego, CA. (ERIC Document Reproduction Service No. ED 406 704)

ABOUT THE EDITOR

Jinyan Huang (Ph.D.) is an associate professor and Ph.D. faculty member at the College of Education, Niagara University. Before coming to Niagara University, he was a linguist and desktop publisher at Lionbridge Technologies in Boston. He had also worked as a university English teacher in the People's Republic of China. He completed his Ph.D. (2007) in cognitive studies (Measurement and TESOL) at Queen's University in Canada. As part of his Ph.D. program, he studied at the Centre for Research in Applied Measurement and Evaluation at the University of Alberta in 2004. He earned his M.A. (2000) in TESOL and also a Graduate Certificate (1999) in TESOL from Brigham Young University.

Dr. Huang's areas of research centre on ESOL learning, assessment, leadership and policy issues. Specifically, he is interested in the following four issues: a) ESOL students' learning challenges and coping strategies; b) factors or level of factors that affect ESOL students' learning outcomes; c) ESOL assessment issues (reliability, validity, and fairness) in schools and universities; and d) the uses of data for supporting ESOL leadership and policies. In today's increasingly multicultural societies, these research interests have practical and policy implications. Such a focus enables Dr. Huang to concentrate on the use of his research expertise in ESOL cognition, generalizability (G-) theory, item response theory (IRT), structural equation modeling (SEM), and hierarchal linear modeling (HLM).

Dr. Huang's recent publications include his book *Understanding Foreign Language Classroom Anxiety* and journal articles published by *Assessing Writing*; *TESOL Journal*; *Language Assessment Quarterly; The Modern Languages Journal; Journal of Quantitative Analysis in Sports; International Journal of Learning and Development; International Journal of Education; International Journal of Humanities and Social Science; International Journal of Business and Social Science; International Journal of Applied Educational Studies; Canadian and International Education; Journal of Instructional Psychology*; and *Education*.

PART 1: CHINESE ESL STUDENTS

In: East Meets West
Editor: Jinyan Huang

ISBN: 978-1-62618-195-3
© 2013 Nova Science Publishers, Inc.

Chapter 1

UNDERSTANDING CHINESE ESL STUDENTS' LEARNING APPROACHES

Jinyan Huang and Peter Cowden*

Niagara University, Lewiston, New York, US

ABSTRACT

Research has indicated that Chinese ESL (CESL) students experience considerable challenges in their academic studies at North American universities. This chapter explores CESL students' academic learning through cultural studies perspectives by examining the concept of identity; cultural and linguistic context; CESL students as quiet and passive learners; different classroom teaching methods experienced in both cultures; surface learners vs. deep learners; different culture worlds; and the concept of social communicative competence. The purpose is to gain a better understanding of CESL students' challenges as well as their learning approaches in the North American universities. It is argued that quiet, passive and surface learners are perhaps incorrect descriptors of CESL students who are studying at North American Universities. Important educational implications are discussed.

INTRODUCTION

Chinese ESL (CESL) students from the People's of China are the largest single group of ESL students studying at North American universities (Canadian Bureau for International Education, 2002; Institute of International Education, 2001). Furthermore, approximately eighty percent of the CESL students currently studying at North American universities are graduate students[1]. They generally have received their undergraduate education in China prior to commencing graduate school in North America. The academic learning of CESL students

---

* Correspondence concerning this chapter should be addressed to Dr. Jinyan Huang at *jhuang@niagara.edu*.
[1] Throughout this chapter, the term 'CESL students' refer to 'CESL graduate students who are from the People's Republic of China and currently studying at North American universities.'

at North American universities has important implications for university administrators and other educators.

Research with ESL students studying at North American universities has indicated that CESL students experience considerable challenges in their academic studies (Chen, 1999; Feng, 1991; Huang, 2004, 2005, 2006; Huang and Klinger, 2006; Liu, 1994; Sun and Chen, 1997; Upton, 1989; Zhong, 1996). All these studies identified both linguistic and cultural factors that affect CESL students' academic studies: their unfamiliarity with the North American culture; their lack of North American academic background; their lack of academic study skills, and their inadequate English proficiency. But none of them has examined CESL students' academic learning through the perspectives of cultural studies, which examines the implications of the social, cultural, philosophical, historical and political contexts for education from a very *critical* perspective.

CESL students are from a very different cultural environment and educational system. They are often stereotyped as quiet, passive and surface by North American instructors (Samuelowicz, 1987; Pratt and Wong, 1999). We would argue that this is a wrong and distorted identity of CESL students. They are not offered equal opportunities both in and outside North American classrooms and they are treated as outsiders or "others".

THE CONCEPT OF IDENTITY

Taylor (1992) defines *identity* as a person's understanding of who s/he is, of her/his fundamental defining characteristics as a human being. And how one defines oneself is partly dependent on the recognition, mis-recognition, or absence of recognition by others. "Non-recognition or mis-recognition can inflict harm; can be a form of oppression, imprisoning someone in a false, distorted and reduced mode of being" (Taylor, 1992, p. 25).

Contemporary conceptions of identity are influenced by postmodern/poststructural/postcolonial writers who reject theoretical discourses which conceptualize identity as a state (which can be measured) rather than as process (Ghosh, 2000). Earlier discussions of identity were located in the area of personality as "a person's essential, continuous self, the internal, subjective concept of oneself as an individual" (Reber, 1985, p. 341). Social *identity* research challenged this individualistic frame and subjective definition of the notion of *identity* as a stabilized factor, an essential personality trait.

Identity is no longer seen as a static, unitary trait. *It* is now seen as being formed in social processes (Krugly-Smolska, 1997). People construct their identities within the social framework.

As such, identities are constantly shifting and renegotiable, and the search for new/modified identities, therefore, is a coping mechanism in the confusion caused by migration and global changes. At the individual level, those who identify with a group can redefine the meaning and norms of group identity (Ghosh, 2000).

Although *identity* is not formed only within race, gender, nationality, class, and sexual preference, those are very important in forming one's identity (Krugly-Smolska, 1997). *Each* person has many "social identities" such as ethnic, sexual, and class identities that develop meaning in people's lives both at the ideological/political and social/*cultural* level. People's multiple identities are not apparent in all contexts and represent different spheres of reality in everyday life. Different ones are important at different times (Ghosh, 2000).

CESL STUDENTS AND THEIR IDENTITY

Two things decide CESL students' identity: how they identify themselves and their identification by North Americans. According to Ghosh (2000), how CESL students identify themselves should be based upon their experiences of the past and present social, cultural and economic relations; and how North Americans define them is influenced by how their differences from the "norm" are viewed and constructed. The norm is based on the physical, cultural and value attributes of the majority or dominant North American culture.

The experiences of CESL students, particularly how they are perceived or identified at North American universities and among their North American peers, have a direct impact on the construction of their identity. At North American universities, administrative people, professors, and staff members are all involved in influencing the construction of CESL students' identity by the way they interact with them and the manner in which they deal with conflicts. What the professor expects, the invisible biases and hidden inequalities in classroom interactions influence how CESL students perceive themselves.

CESL Students as Surface Learners

Marton and Saljo (1976) conducted the early studies on CESL students' learning approaches. They compared CESL students with Westerns learners and identified the former as surface learners and the latter deep learners. In their research they simply asked the students to read some written passages and then describe what they did while reading the passages. CESL students, in their study, reported trying to memorize the phrases or words used by the author. More recently several studies indicate that Western instructors believe that CESL students tend to take a shallow approach to learning, they want to rote learn and do not want to think (Samuelowicz, 1987; Pratt and Wong, 1999). Actually these researchers just misperceive Chinese approaches to learning. What they do is just simply ask CESL students to read some passages or answer some questions and then classify them as surface learners (a very "surface" research approach). As a result, many Western educators now believe that CESL students engage in memorization and are not interested in deep understanding (Pratt and Wong, 1999). We would argue that CESL students use memorization as a path to understanding and vice versa. Memorization and understanding are related to each other. CESL students may engage in strategies that appear to be surface oriented but actually are deep oriented (Biggs, 1987; Kember and Gow, 1991; Marton, Dall'Alba, and Kun, 1996).

CESL Students as Quiet and Passive Learners

CESL students are frequently characterized as passive learners at North American classrooms (Chen, 1985; Feng, 1991; Upton, 1989). They are not actively asking and answering questions, and participating in classroom discussions. We would argue that North American classrooms did not produce desirable learning environment for CESL students.

First, North American classrooms produce an informal and disrespectful learning environment. CESL students often feel uncomfortable with the students' behaviors at North American classrooms. They have a negative reaction toward North American students' behaviors (Chen, 1985; Upton, 1989). Students can be late for class. They often ask teacher questions or make jokes in class. All these behaviors are considered rude and disrespectful in Chinese classrooms. In North American classrooms students can challenge the teacher at any time by interrupting the teachers and ask them questions, which make CESL students feel that students do not show any respect for their teachers, because in Chinese culture teachers are considered as authorities and they should gain respect from their students. So this learning atmosphere stops CESL students from active learning in North American classrooms.

Second, North American culture excludes CESL students from North Americans in the classrooms. Due to their different cultural background, CESL students are not familiarized themselves with North American culture. North American culture has become a major source for demonstrating examples, discussing topics, and cheerful jokes in the classroom. Undoubtedly, CESL students have problems understanding and participating in classroom interactions. They are in fact treated unequally as their North American peers.

Finally, CESL students are wrongly labeled as passive or inactive learners in North American classrooms. They are "passive" perhaps because they have no access to classroom interactions. They are "inactive" perhaps because they are ignored or forgotten by the North Americans in the classroom. Thus they are treated as a different group of "others" in the classroom: quiet, passive, inactive, and struggling students.

A FALSE AND DISTORTED IDENTITY

CESL students at North American universities are often stereotyped as quiet, passive, surface, reserved and non-assertive, which is a wrong and distorted identity. This is related to a larger problem of "othering," the tendency to perceive outsiders to North American society in particular, or Western culture in general, solely through comparison and contrast to what "we" value and how "we" act. As Said (1979) points out, treating the "other" as opposite is the worst form of stereotyping, because it invalidates the "other" as a self-proclaiming entity. The formation of this false identity of CESL students thus indicates a lack of understanding and validation of Chinese culture and the teaching methodology employed in the classroom.

Different Culture Worlds

Chinese culture has a great influence on the Chinese people today. While there are many ideologies that may influence; Confucian philosophy can have a strong impact on the Chinese people's viewpoint, way of thinking and behaviors. Confucius' philosophy on learning, for example, can be summarized as "effortful learning, behavioral reform, pragmatic learning, acquisition of essential knowledge, and respectful learning" (Tweed and Lehman, 2002, p. 91).

Confucius stressed the importance of hard work. He believed that one's success mainly came from his hard work not his ability. He also believed that "behavior reform is a central goal of education because virtuous behavior can ensure individual success and societal harmony" (p. 92). Confucius valued pragmatic learning. He viewed the goal of learning as to competently conduct oneself within a civil service job. He stressed the acquisition of essential knowledge and respectful learning. He taught his students to respect and obey authorities. He once said that "to honor those higher than ourselves is the highest expression of the sense of justice" (Confucius, 1947, p. 332).

Chinese culture places an emphasis on harmony and respect for authorities. Therefore, CESL students are usually reluctant to share their feelings or emotions, express their opinions or oppositions to anyone, especially to authority figures. Thus instead of emphasizing personal rights and assertive communication, CESL students tend to emphasize the importance of patience, harmony, respect and deference. Chinese culture tends to place a high value on team efforts or collectivity whereas North American culture tends to emphasize individualism. CESL students are also modest about their accomplishments.

Many of them feel uncomfortable with the individualism and the competitiveness associated with the North American culture (Lin and Yi, 1997). Or stated in another way: while individualism and the competitiveness may exist in China; many of them may feel uncomfortable with the degree of individualism and the competitiveness associated with the North American culture.

CESL students at North American universities often struggle between the balance of acculturation and maintaining their own culture. The process of acculturation and adjustment can be stressful. The differences between the two cultures can cause a student to experience significant intrapersonal and interpersonal problems and conflicts. According to Lin and Yi (1997), many CESL students experience the following: pressure from academic demands, language barriers, financial concerns, performance anxiety, depression, loneliness, homesickness, relationship problems, non-assertiveness, individualism and bicultural conflicts, stereotyping, prejudice, discrimination and paranoia.

Different Classroom Teaching Methods

The discourse of participation is highly valued, promulgated and practiced by North American teachers (Cortazzi and Jin, 1996). This discourse is often seen in China as exotic and students often become confused with what the teacher expects of them in a seemingly unsupportive environment where conversations, discussions, debates and participation become the dominant mode of teaching (Sun, 1990; Wan, 1997).

Originating from the Western culture of learning, the discourse becomes problematic in the Chinese educational contexts, where the authoritative discourse is stressed and the primary role of a teacher as an authority is to teach while the major role of a student is to receive, absorb, and digest the knowledge transmitted by the teacher (Cortazzi and Jin, 1996; Craig, 1995; Wan, 1997).

Fu (1991) argues that the roles of the teacher are defined and interpreted differently in North American and Chinese cultures. In Chinese culture there is lack of the spirit of equality in the classrooms. Teachers are regarded not only as authorities in their field of study but also students' moral mentor. While in North American classrooms, there is an equal relationship between teachers and students. So Chinese teachers are always very serious and focus on lecturing and North American teachers often use humor and varied, informal teaching methods in classroom. Difference in classroom teaching methodology has become the biggest cultural difference for CESL students and North American teachers' different teaching methods cause considerable challenges for them in their classroom learning process (Chen, 1985; Upton, 1989). As identified in Huang's (2005) study, the following characteristics related to North American classroom teaching methodology negatively affects CESL students' classroom learning: 1) too much group work and student participation; 2) failure to follow the textbook; 3) poor lecture organization, and lack of lecture summary in particular; and 4) lack of blackboard writing (Huang, 2005).

Those studies argue that CESL students are not used to North American teaching methods and so they have difficulties in classroom learning, which implies that they would have no challenges at all if they were familiarized themselves with North American classroom teaching methods. But if we take one step further to discuss this issue; it is actually a question of an unequal relationship between CESL students and North American professors and peers.

First of all, we disagree with Fu's position that in North American classrooms, there is an equal relationship between teachers and students. In North American classrooms, there also exists inequality. North American professors have power or authority over CESL students and North American students have more privileges than CESL students.

Group work and student participation are the dominant mode of teaching in North American classrooms. In considering the use of group work and student participation in the classroom, we need to ask the following questions: what are students really doing and how are they feeling working in groups? Are these methods used correctly? And which students are really participating? Our personal conversations with CESL students about their own North American classroom learning experience show that there is too much complaint from CESL students about student participation and group work in North American classrooms. For example, some North American students waste other students' time by just talking about nonsense in the classroom and the teacher seems enjoying his/her meaningless talk. Sometimes group-work is not used correctly by the North American professors either. For example, CESL students are often grouped with CESL students or other ESL students and their "otherness" or different identity is further confirmed in the classroom. Whether this is a North American uniqueness is unclear. Also, while this may have some positive benefits; it can also lead to isolation.

The structuring or organizing of a lecture is an essential aspect of its comprehensibility and effective lecture preparation and delivery can be arranged under the following three stages: 1) the beginning; 2) the body; and 3) the closing (Chaudron and Richards, 1986; Diamond, Sharp, and Ory, 1983). In the beginning stage, the lecturer usually relates lecture content to previous class material, mentions the background of the current lecture, or gives students a brief introduction of the content of the current lecture. In the body of the lecture, there is some flexibility for the lecturer to present the content. The lecturer can either decide the main points and explain them clearly to the listeners or organize the material in some logical order such as "cause-effect," "time-sequential," etc. During the lecture the lecturer may ask some questions to check on students' understanding of the lecture or ask them to make their comments. In the last stage of the lecture, the lecturer may briefly summarize the content of the lecture or reemphasize what he expects the students to learn from the lecture. But many CESL students comment that their North American teachers, compared with their teachers in China, are poorer classroom managers or organizers, and they do not usually know how to effectively teach their classes (Huang, 2005; Upton, 1989). CESL students often get confused about what they should learn about a lecture. Upton (1989) interviewed a CESL student and made the following comments:

> One Chinese student I interviewed said that she felt frustrated because she was not always sure what exactly the teachers wanted her to know. When she asked a teacher to help her out, his response of "You don't have to understand everything" really confused her (Upton, 1989, p. 25).

To sum up, North American professors have the power to choose what to teach, and how to teach in particular. When they are choosing a North American method to teach a class, they actually ignore their CESL students, the language minority students in the classroom. North American professors do not intentionally ignore CESL students. They are lacking the knowledge, resources, or expertise to include Chinese cultural components and CESL students in the classroom. It is a solution found in the training of our teachers and the acceptance of this need by the educational system. As a result, CESL students' prior educational experience is devalued and their voices about their learning strategies and preferences are not heard. Therefore they are not offered the equal opportunities and, ultimately, they can hardly gain equal in-group memberships of the classroom learning community as their North American peers.

CESL Students in Classroom Communities

In North American classrooms, teachers often ask students to discuss current events; comment on TV shows; and write newspaper article critiques (Alvermann, Moon, and Hagood, 1999; Buckingham, 1998; Huang, 2005; Stevens, 2001). North American students have grown up in this cultural context and established their in-group membership with other North Americans. They can talk about their past social experience. They have no difficulty in understanding classroom discussions and sharing their own social experience. CESL students, however, have not grown up in this cultural context; surely have difficulty in comprehending lectures at North American classrooms. According to a study by Huang (2005) on the challenges experienced by CESL students in understanding academic lectures at an American university, about 80% of the participants comment that their American teachers use examples or situations that happen only in American culture while lecturing and strongly agree that the use of unfamiliar examples or situations caused great challenges for them in understanding class lectures. That is to say, CESL students have great difficulty being included in the social worlds of their North American counterparts within the classrooms. The use of examples or situations that happen only in North American culture in the classrooms delights only the North American students, allowing them to display and construct their "identities, knowledge, interests, past experiences, sense of humor, and sociocultural affiliations (Duff, 2002)." However, it excludes CESL students from the classroom community. They are treated as outsiders of the classroom learning community. In the classroom, CESL students do not have equal opportunities to speak and they speak only when they are asked to. Having fewer North American cultural reference points that might help their comprehension, they usually have considerable challenges understanding what their North American classmates are talking about. But if CESL students ask for explanations and try to join the discussions in class the North Americans might further confirm their difference and "otherness". Silence protects them from humiliation but it does not help them gain access to the valued cultural capital and practices of their North American peers. So in class CESL students are seen as marginal participants, shy, communicatively incompetent, and uninterested in the local culture, with identities thus defined by their nonparticipation and disengagement (Wenger, 1998). On the contrary, CESL students have their own senses of humor, their culture alignments, their talents, their social affiliations, and intelligence. All those are not valued and thus become invisible and inaccessible to others in North American classroom communities.

CESL Students in Outside-Classroom Communities

Social communicative competence is conceptualized as a multitude of *social* communication skills that increase a person's *social* communicative effectiveness. These communication skills include listening, initiating *social* contacts, asking and responding to questions, or expressing one's point of view without offending others (Mathur and Rutherford, 1994). A person with those social communication skills is capable of initiating and maintaining positive *social* interactions, developing friendships, establishing collaborative networks, and coping effectively with their *social* environment. In contrast, lack of *social* communication skills has been identified as one of the major predictors of low self-esteem, peer rejection, *social* maladjustment, mental health problems, and delinquency (Asher and Wheeler, 1985; Elliott and Gresham, 1993).

What is the content of North American students' social communications in outside-classroom communities? Much of what students read, write, and talk about out of school today is *culture,* which means North American students' social life is linked to North American culture (Asselin, 2001).

Forming and maintaining friendships, taking the initiative in conversations and a willingness to converse with native North American students are all important to CESL students' social communications in outside-classroom communities, according to Myles, Qian, and Cheng (2002). CESL students, however, have not grown up in the North American cultural context, so they obviously will have difficulty in communicating and establishing in-group memberships with their North American peers. In outside-classroom communities, CESL students feel difficult to socialize themselves with North American people due to their lack of North American culture. They share no common interest with North Americans and thus can hardly make real friends with them (Feng, 1991; Sun and Chen, 1997).

The results of Feng's (1991) study indicate that CESL students experience peer rejection and report feelings of loneliness and *social* isolation at North American universities. They share no common topics and interest with North American students is a considerable challenge for CESL students at North American universities. North Americans often talk about football and baseball, for example. But CESL students have no idea about North American sports. Due to two different cultures, CESL students often avoid participating in social activities in North America. They feel hard to make real North American friends. There is a lack of mutual understanding between CESL students and their North American peers.

In addition, in the same study, Feng (1991) talks about holidays as an important part of North American culture. North Americans and Chinese people have very different holidays to celebrate each year. In North America, Christmas, Thanksgiving, Easter, and Halloween are very important holidays. North American people have different traditions for different holidays and their ways to celebrate different holidays are also different. While in China, people celebrate the Spring Festival, the Dragon Boat Festival, the Mid-Autumn Festival, and some other festivals. When the North Americans are celebrating their holidays, CESL students cannot feel that kind of holiday atmosphere and they often isolate themselves from the North Americans. When Chinese holidays come, they have to go to school. They are also far from their parents and friends. They cannot feel the right kind of Chinese holiday atmosphere either. In that sense, CESL students at North American universities cannot really enjoy any kind of holidays, which increases their homesickness and isolation.

Finally, Feng (1991) mentions religion as another big problem that bothers CESL students in North America. In China people are educated not to believe in God, while in North America religion is an important part of culture. CESL students feel very much concerned about how to deal with religion in North America. In some parts of North America, going to church is the only thing people do on Sundays. The following report by a CESL student reflects some CESL students' concerns about religion in North America:

> This city is very religious. But in China, few people are interested in religion. We grew up in a communist society. We have been educated by communist doctrine since we were little. Of course many people here are friendly, and willing to help foreign students. But, they often talk about God, and try to convince you to believe in God, which make many of us uncomfortable…
>
> Although host families can help you understand American culture. I think they are often too religious. They are so much interested in religion. They give you Bible, and want you to spend time reading the Bible. On Sundays, they take you to local church. I don't like that (Feng, 1991, p. 10)

Feng's (1991) study analyzes how cultural differences create challenges for CESL students in their academic learning process at North American universities. But the analysis is limited to very surface understanding of the role of North American culture in CESL students' learning process in North America. For example, Feng (1991) comments that CESL students have difficulties in communicating socially with their North American peers outside the classroom and their difficulties come from their unfamiliarity with the North American culture, which means CESL students should totally forget their Chinese culture and soon become North Americanized. The North American culture actually plays a very negative role in CESL students' outside classroom social communications with North American people. North American culture, as the dominant culture, excludes CESL students as a group of different people from "other" places.

Chinese culture is not very much valued in North America. As a matter of fact, CESL students at North American universities are deprived of their basic rights as human beings: the right to make true friends, the right to enjoy holidays, and the right to be treated equally as members of the community, not as different "others".

As a result, it can be argued that the North-American academia is not culturally inclusive enough due to the fact that CESL students are in North America which is a totally different culture. It is very likely that they will not be able to make true friends and enjoy holidays as they could do while in China. In this sense, such rights have been deprived.

CONCLUSION

It is argued in this chapter that CESL students are from a very different cultural and linguistic context. North American educators should try to create a more inclusive learning environment for this group of culturally and linguistically different students (Duff, 2002).

There are many challenges faced by CESL students in North America. It has been demonstrated that linguistic and cultural factors affect CESL students' academic studies: their unfamiliarity with the North American culture; their lack of North American academic background; their lack of academic study skills, and their inadequate English proficiency all add to their challenges. One should note that the use of examples or situations that happen only in the North American culture should not be used excessively in the classroom. Rather, these examples or situations should be part of an inclusive multicultural perspective.

Further, we need to help CESL students understand North American culture and encourage them to actively participate in classroom discussions. We should also encourage CESL students to bring elements of their culture into classroom discussions. By doing this, they can gradually gain equal in-group memberships as their North American peers[2].

REFERENCES

Alvermann, D., Moon, J., and Hagood, M. (1999). *Popular culture in the classroom.* Newark, DE and Chicago: International Reading Association and the National Reading Conference.

Asher, S.R., and Wheeler, V.A. (1985). Children's loneliness: A comparison of rejected and neglected peer status. *Journal of Consulting and Clinical Psychology, 53,* 500-505.

Asselin, M. (2001). Teaching literacy from and with popular culture. *Teacher Librarian 28,* 47-49.

Biggs, J. B. (1987). *Student approaches to learning and studying.* Melbourne: Australian Council for Educational Research.

Buckingham, D. (Ed.). (1998). *Teaching popular culture: Beyond radical pedagogy.* London: University College Press.

Canadian Bureau for International Education. (2002, April 15). *International student numbers hit record high, but Canada offers dwindling support for African students.* Retrieved October 28, 2002 from the World Wide Web: http://www.cbie.ca/news/index_ e.cfm?folder=releasesandpage=rel_2002-04-15_e.

Chaudron, C., and Richards, J. C. (1986). The effect of discourse markers on the comprehension of lectures. *Applied Linguistics, 7,* 113-127.

Chen, C. P. (1999). Common stressors among international college students: Research and counseling implications. *Journal of College Conseling, 2,* 49-65.

Chen, T. H. (1985). *Cultural differences in classrooms: A comparison of Chinese and US schooling.* Unpublished manuscript.

Confucius. (1947). The wisdom of Confucius. In S. Commins and R. N. Linscott (Eds.), *Man and man: The social philosophers* (pp. 323-358). New York: Random House. (Original work published ca. 479 B. C. E.).

---

[2] This article was originally published in *Canadian and International Education*.

Cortazzi, M., and Jin, L. X. (1996). Cultures of learning: Language classrooms in China. In H. Coleman (Ed.), *Society and the language classroom* (pp. 169-206). Melbourne: Cambridge University Press.

Craig, B. A. (1995). Boundary discourse and the authority of knowledge in the second-language classroom: A social-constructionist approach. In J. E. Alatis et al., (Eds.), *Georgetown University round table on language and linguistics, 1995* (pp. 40-54). Washington D. C.: Georgetown University Press.

Diamond, N. A., Sharp, G. and Ory, J. C. (1983). *Improving your lecturing.* Office of Instructional and Management Services, University of Illinois at Urbana-Champaign.

Duff, P. A. (2002). Pop culture and ESL students: Intertextuality, identity, and participation in classroom discussions. *Journal of Adolescent and Adult Literacy, 45,* 482-487.

Elliott, S.N., and Gresham, F. M. (1993). *Social* skills interventions for children. Special Issue: *Social*-skills and intervention with children and adolescents. *Behavior Modification, 1,* 287-313.

Fu, D. L. (1991). A process classroom through the eyes of an outsider. *Language Arts, 68,* 121-123.

Feng, J. H. (1991). *The adaptation of Students from the People's Republic of China to an American Academic Culture.* Reports (ERIC Document Reproduction Service No. ED 329 833).

Ghosh, R. (2000). Identity and social integration: Girls from a minority ethno-cultural group in Canada. *McGill Journal of Education 35,* 279-296.

Huang, J. (2004). Voices from Chinese students: Professors' use of English affects academic listening. *College Student Journal, 38*(2), 212-223.

Huang, J. (2005). Challenges of academic listening in English: Reports by Chinese students. *College Student Journal, 39*(3), 553-569.

Huang, J. (2006). English abilities for academic listening: How confident are Chinese students? *College Student Journal, 40*(1), 218-226.

Huang, J., and Klinger, D. (2006). Chinese graduate students at North American universities: Learning challenges and coping strategies. *The Canadian and International Education Journal, 35*(2*)*, 48-61.

Institute of International Education. (2001, June 15). *98/99 opendoors on the Web.* [Selections from the book], New York. Retrieved June 15, 2002 from the World Wide Web: http://www.opendoorsweb.org/Lead%20 Stories/international_studs.htm.

Kember, D., and Gow, L. (1991). A challenge to the anecdotal stereotype of the Asian student. *Studies in Higher Education, 16,* 117-128.

Krugly-Smolska, E. (1997). Global and local challenges of/to the post-modern: Implications for education. *Canadian and International Education, 26 (2),* 1-7.

Lin, J. G., and Yi, J. K. (1997). Asian international students' adjustment: Issues and program suggestions. *College Student Journal, 31,* 473-479.

Liu, D. L. (1994). Deep sociocultural transfer and its effect on second language speakers' communication. *Paper presented at the annual meeting of the Teachers of English to Speakers of Other Languages,* Maltimore, MD.

Mathur, S. R., and Rutherford, R. B. (1994). Teaching conversational skills to delinquent youth. *Behavioral Disorders, 19,* 294-305.

Marton, F., Dall'Alba, G., and Kun, T. L. (1996). Memorizing and understanding: The keys to the paradox? In D. A. Watkins and J. B. Biggs (Eds.), *The Chinese learner: Cultural, psychological, and contextual influences* (pp. 69-84). Hong Kong: Comparative Education Research Center.

Marton, F., and Saljo, R. (1976). On qualitative differences in learning: Outcome and process. *British Journal of Educational Psychology, 46,* 4-11.

Myles, J., Qian, J., and Cheng, L. (2002) International and new immigrant students' adaptations to the social and cultural life at a Canadian university. In S. Bond and C. Bowry (Eds.) *Connections and Complexities: The Internationalization of Canadian Higher Education,* Occasional Papers in *Higher Education,* Vol, 11, Winnipeg, Center for Research and Development in Higher Education.

Pratt, D. D., and Wong, K. M. (1999). Chinese conceptions of "effective teaching" in Hong Kong: Towards culturally sensitive evaluation of teaching. *International Journal of Lifelong Education, 18,* 241-258.

Reber, A. (1985). *The Penguin dictionary of psychology.* Harmondsworth: Penguin.

Said, E. W. (1979). *Orientalism.* New York: Vintage Books.

Samuelowicz, K. (1987). Learning problems of overseas students: Two sides of a story. *Higher Education Research and Development, 6,* 121-134.

Stevens, L. (2001). South Park and society: Instructional and curricular implications of popular culture in the classroom. *Journal of Adolescent and Adult Literacy, 44,* 548-555.

Sun, G. Y. (1990). English teaching in China. *ELT Newsletter: Teaching English in China, 21,* 76-82.

Sun, W., and Chen, G. M. (1997). *Dimensions of difficulties Mainland Chinese students encounter in the United States.* Paper presented at the 6th International Conference in Cross-Cultural Communication, Tempe, AZ. (ERIC Document Reproduction Service No. ED 408 635).

Taylor, C. (1992). The politics of recognition. In A. Gutman (Ed.), *Multiculturalism and the "politics of recognition"* (pp. 25-74). Princeton, New Jersey: Princeton University Press.

Tweed R. G., and Lehman, D. R. (2002). Learning considered within a cultural context. *American Psychologist,* Vol, 57, No. 2, 89-99.

Upton, T. A. (1989). Chinese students, American universities, and cultural confrontation. *MinneTESOL Journal, 7,* 9-28.

Wan, Z. X. (1997). Observation on teaching style of native-speaking teachers in Chinese ELT classrooms. *ELT Newsletter: Teaching English in China, 29,* 101-104.

Wenger, E. (1998). *Communities of practice: Learning, meaning, and identity.* Cambridge, England: Cambridge University Press.

Zhong, M. (1996). Chinese students and scholars in the US: An intercultural adaptation process. *Paper presented at the 82nd Annual Meeting of the Speech Communication Association,* San Diego, CA. (ERIC Document Reproduction Service No. ED 406 704).

In: East Meets West
Editor: Jinyan Huang

ISBN: 978-1-62618-195-3
© 2013 Nova Science Publishers, Inc.

Chapter 2

UNDERSTANDING CHINESE ESL STUDENTS' ACADEMIC ANXIETY

Jinyan Huang[1,] and Shuangli Su[2]*

[1]Niagara University, Lewiston, New York, US
[2]Untested Ideas Research Center, Niagara Falls, New York, US

ABSTRACT

This chapter reports a qualitative study which examined whether or not four Chinese ESL (CESL) Ph.D. students were experiencing high levels of academic anxiety at two North American universities and if so, their perceptions of the factors contributing to their academic anxiety, the impact of academic anxiety on their learning, and their strategies for coping with academic anxiety. The results show that two participants were experiencing high levels of academic anxiety. Majors that involve more language usage, such as education, political studies, and religious studies, seem to cause greater levels of academic anxiety than those majors that rely more on graphs, tables, numbers and symbols, such as mathematics, biology, and chemistry. The major sources of high levels of academic anxiety, as reported by these two participants, are financial difficulties, language barriers, cultural differences, being away from family and friends, and difficulty in finding an employment. Academic anxiety decreases their self-confidence and also has a negative impact on their academic learning, social life, and personal feelings. Important implications are discussed.

INTRODUCTION

The number of ESL students has more than doubled since the 1980s and has recently grown significantly at North American universities; Chinese ESL (CESL) students from the People's Republic of China (PRC) represent the single largest group of ESL students (Canadian Bureau for International Education, 2009; Institute of International Education, 2010). Further, CESL graduate students make up approximately eighty percent of CESL

---

[*] Correspondence concerning this chapter should be addressed to Dr. Jinyan Huang at *jhuang@niagara.edu*.

students currently studying at North American universities. These CESL graduate students have generally received their undergraduate education in PRC. The academic learning experience of this group of CESL graduate students has important educational implications for university administrators and educators (Huang and Klinger, 2006).

CESL students are from a very different educational system and cultural background. Previous research has indicated that there are considerable challenges faced by CESL graduate students in their academic studies at North American universities, e.g., their unfamiliarity with North American culture, their inadequate English proficiency, their social and emotional challenges, their financial difficulties, etc. (Chen, 1999; Huang and Brown, 2009; Huang, 2004, 2005, 2009; Huang and Klinger, 2006; Lin, 2002; Liu, 1994; Myles, Qian and Cheng, 2002; Wan, 2001; Zhong, 1996). For example, Chinese culture is very different from the culture of North America and the cultural differences have a negative impact on their academic studies (Huang and Brown, 2009; Huang and Rinaldo, 2009). This is because students from different cultures learn in different ways, and may differ in their learning styles, self-expressions and communication styles (Bennett, 1999). Potentially, all these challenges may contribute to anxiety for CESL graduate students; and consequently anxiety negatively affects their academic learning at North American universities (Feng, 1991; Huang, 1998; Sun and Chen, 1997; Upton, 1989).

The questions of whether or not CESL graduate students are really experiencing high levels of anxiety in their academic studies and if so, what factors cause their anxiety and how anxiety affects their academic learning at North American universities merit closer examination, on which limited research has been conducted.

LITERATURE REVIEW

CESL graduate students face both challenges and anxiety when studying at North American universities. However, these two concepts are not completely separated in the literature. For example, major challenges faced by CESL graduate students include financial burdens, changes in culture, legal frustrations, leaving their families, differences in classroom instruction, and anxiety (Huang and Rinaldo, 2009; Huang and Klinger, 2006). Anxiety has then become a major challenge for CESL graduate students (Huang and Klinger, 2006). Furthermore, not only is anxiety a challenge itself, but it is argued that anxiety can be caused by the plethora of other challenges that CESL graduate students face on a day to day basis. For this reason, the challenges and causes contributing to anxiety merit closer examination.

Cultural Context

Academic learning differs depending on the cultural context, as argued by Tweed and Lehman (2002). They proposed a Confucian-Socratic framework to analyze the impact different cultural contexts have on academic learning. Confucius (551-479 BC), an Eastern exemplar, valued behavioral reform, effortful and respectful learning, and pragmatic attainment of necessary knowledge (Tweed and Lehman, 2002). "Effort-focused conceptions of learning, pragmatic orientations to learning, and acceptance of behavioral reform as an academic goal" (p. 93) are the trademarks of Confucian-oriented learning. On the other hand, Socrates (469-399 BC), a Western exemplar, valued the evaluation of others' knowledge, the questioning of both his own and others' beliefs, self-generated knowledge, and teaching by establishing doubt. Socratic-oriented learning can be described as "overt and private questioning, expression of personal hypotheses, and a desire for self-directed tasks" (p. 93).

These two philosophies can be looked to when studying the differences between the Chinese culture and the North American culture. While Confucian philosophy has had a strong impact on Chinese people's viewpoints, ways of thinking, behaviors, and experiences; North American students and professors are more influenced by Socratic beliefs. Confucius believed that hard work, rather than ability, contributed most to success. He also asserted that "behavior reform is a central goal of education because virtuous behavior can ensure individual success and societal harmony" (Tweed and Lehman, 2002, p. 92). By obeying and respecting authorities, one exhibits "the highest expression of the sense of justice" (Confucius, 1947, p. 332). The primary goal of pragmatic learning of essential knowledge was to provide individuals with the ability to perform civil service jobs competently. Chinese students who come to North American universities often bring a Confucian-oriented perspective to their learning, while their professors and peers tend to demonstrate a Socratic orientation. Western cultures and beliefs are not familiar to Chinese students; and this unfamiliarity, not surprisingly, causes them to be uncomfortable with North American culture and the North American learning environment. These feelings of unease are especially prevalent for those students whose studies focus on the humanities and social sciences (Huang and Rinaldo, 2009; Huang and Klinger, 2006). Financial difficulties and insufficient English proficiency magnify these difficulties and further reduces these students' ability to participate in academic and social activities (Feng, 1991; Huang and Klinger, 2006).

Language Barriers

Language is an obvious challenge to CESL graduate students. They have difficulties in understanding academic lectures, American idioms and jokes, and in taking notes (Feng, 1991; Huang, 2004, 2005, 2006; Huang and Rinaldo, 2009). The English language problem was identified as the biggest obstacle in the process of CESL graduate students' intercultural adjustment although they came to the United States with high TOEFL (Test of English as a Foreign Language) and GRE (Graduate Record Examination) scores (Sun and Chen, 1997). Poor English proficiency hinders their understanding and has a strong negative impact on their communication with North American professors and peers (Huang and Klinger, 2006). Further, poor English proficiency was cited as the major reason that CESL students, in North America, rated their first-year academic learning as "not enjoyable" (Huang, 1998).

Instructional Differences

North American teachers' different instructional styles, as discussed by Huang and Rinaldo (2009), affect CESL graduate students' classroom learning. For example, in North American classrooms, student participation is encouraged; teachers usually regard themselves as students' facilitators of learning but not their authorities of knowledge. They can admit their ignorance on a topic and give students' freedom to express their different ideas. However, CESL graduate students are used to teachers' point-by-point lectures and therefore, expect their North American teachers to give detailed explanations of every topic and to put the key points or outlines on the blackboard in order for them to take detailed notes. When their expectations are not met, they tend to think that their North American teachers are not as resourceful and responsible as their teachers back in China. But actually it is also a cultural difference.

Instruction is primarily lecture format in Chinese classroom, whereas North American teachers tend to implement critical thinking and discussion into their classrooms (Huang and Klinger, 2006). Chinese classrooms and instruction are often formatted in a formal, step-by-step manner, while the North American classroom is often casual and informal.

The teacher is the driving force behind Chinese classroom instruction, whereas in North America the student tends to also play a major role in the learning process. Further, North American teachers expect their students to do extensive reading and look for related information on their own outside of class (Upton, 1989).

Financial Burden

Huang and Klinger (2006) found financial burdens to be one of the top three negative factors impacting CESL graduate students' academic studies. Financial support in the form of scholarships, fellowships, teaching and research assistantships from the North American universities and the tuition fees as well as other expenses have become the most important criteria for CESL students from PRC when choosing North American graduate schools (Huang and Rinaldo, 2009). Students who do not receive full scholarship face the burden of paying tuition, while also supporting themselves and possible their family financially. Even when students do receive full scholarships, the financial burden is still unavoidable as students are required to maintain minimum grade levels in order to secure their scholarships and funding (Huang and Klinger, 2006). Feng (1991) further indicated that CESL students' financial situations have a negative impact on their academic achievement, English language skill improvement, as well as their participation in social activities.

Legal Issues

CESL graduate students face residency issues and the need for visas (Huang and Rinaldo, 2009). For example, "maintaining a legal status in America is a very important rule for international students, especially after September 11, 2001. Because many CESL graduate students in social sciences choose research topics that have a Chinese context, they need to go back to China regularly to attend conferences and collect data. However, because of the strict immigration laws, these students have to re-apply for a U.S. visa each time in order to re-enter America and many CESL graduate students have been declined re-admittance. This has a profoundly negative influence on them as well as others seeking to complete American degrees" (pp. 6-7). Further, obtaining the visas needed to visit home also proves difficult and contributes to emotional challenges as CESL graduate students are separated from friends and family at home in China.

Social and Emotional Challenges

Often times, CESL graduate students find it hard to make friends and communicate effectively with professors and peers in North America (Huang and Rinaldo, 2009; Huang and Klinger, 2006). Language barriers and financial difficulties only increase the problem, making it difficult for CESL students to participate in social activities and campus functions. Loneliness and anxiety are the two major emotional challenges that CESL graduate students face (Huang and Rinaldo, 2009; Huang and Klinger, 2006). Loneliness comes from substantial distance between the Chinese students and their loved ones. Their parents, families and friends often remain in China while the students study in North America. They have to experience a "long affective torment" (Huang and Rinaldo, 2009, p. 10).

Further, they are experiencing a high level of academic anxiety which negatively affected their academic study, as commented by one participant in Huang and Rinaldo (2009) study: "When I first started my graduate program, I was very anxious about finishing my assignments on time. I also worried about writing course papers. In class I was anxious about participating class discussions, and sometimes, being asked to answer questions. In the following years I worried about writing my thesis and defending my thesis. Currently I worry about finding a job. Anxiety, as a factor, has negative impact on my graduate study here" (p. 10).

Anxiety and Academic Anxiety

Spielberger (1983) defined "anxiety" as "the subjective feeling of tension, apprehension, nervousness, and worry associated with an arousal of the autonomic nervous system." It can refer to not only a person's stable personality but also his transitory emotional state. Accordingly, two anxiety constructs have been developed: trait anxiety and state anxiety. Because they are more likely to interpret a wider range of situations as threatening; people with high trait anxiety tend to produce state anxiety more frequently than those with low trait anxiety (Head and Knight, 1988).

Anxiety is a common phenomenon in people's learning process. It prevents learners from completing academic tasks successfully, and so it interrupts learning. Academic anxiety then refers to the anxiety that occurs during the learning process (Garcia, 1998). High levels of academic anxiety have a debilitating effect on concept learning, academic performance, and environmental adaptation, and so leading lower learning efficiency (Clark and Schwartz, 1989). Thus, high levels of academic anxiety impede academic learning and achievement.

CESL graduate students' inadequate English proficiency, their financial difficulties, their lack of North American educational and academic cultural understanding, together with their social and emotional challenges and some other possible factors may increase their anxiety levels, which could adversely affect their academic learning at North American universities. However, little research has examined the questions of whether or not CESL graduate students are really experiencing high levels of academic anxiety and if so, what factors cause their academic anxiety and how it affects their learning at North American universities.

Considering the large number of CESL graduate students studying in North America and the limited research conducted in the area, it is of great importance to examine these questions.

METHODOLOGY

The purpose of this study was to hear the voices of four CESL graduate students about their North American academic learning experiences, focusing on academic anxiety and its causes and impact on their learning. Specifically, it was to examine whether or not they experience high levels of academic anxiety and if so, their perceptions of a) the factors contributing to their academic anxiety, b) the impact of academic anxiety on their learning, and c) their strategies for dealing with academic anxiety.

Random purposive sampling strategy was be used to select participants due to the fact that it adds credibility to the study (Gay and Airasian, 2003). A pool of 10 participants from two North American universities was selected. After determining that four interviews could reasonably be dealt with for the purpose of this study, four participants from the original pool were randomly selected to participate. Four CESL Ph.D. students from PRC, currently studying at two North American universities, were invited to participate in this study.

At the time of the interview, Participant A (female) was a fifth year Ph.D. student majoring in cognitive studies; Participant B (female) was in her third year working towards a Ph.D. in biology and chemistry; Participant C (male) was a fifth year mathematics Ph.D. student; and Participant D (female) was in her second year of study for a Ph.D. in organic chemistry.

Semi-structured interviews were conducted via telephone between the principal researcher and the participants. These interviews allowed the participants to describe their academic learning experience, identifying their perceptions of their level of academic anxiety, the factors contributing to their academic anxiety and how, if at all, it affects their academic learning at these two North American universities.

To avoid any miscommunications, interviews were conducted in the participants' native language, Chinese, and then transcribed and translated into English. The translated transcriptions were further checked through back-translation.

The participants' responses were then sorted, categorized, and analyzed, to determine if they faced high levels of academic anxiety, and if so, what factors contributed to academic anxiety, how it affected their learning, and the strategies they have developed to cope with academic anxiety. Responses relevant to these questions were grouped together and then categorized and analyzed according to the recurring themes.

MAJOR FINDINGS

The results of the interviews are summarized below. As described above, the following three questions were investigated: a) Whether or not the participants are experiencing high levels of academic anxiety? b) If so, what are the causes of their academic anxiety? And c) what impact does academic anxiety have on their learning. Further, the strategies they have developed to cope with academic anxiety were examined.

Whether or Not Participants Are Experiencing High Levels of Academic Anxiety?

The answer to this question could be both yes and no. Participants *A* and *C* reported that they were experiencing high levels of academic anxiety. Participant *A*, who was a female Ph.D. student studying cognition in her fifth year, reported that "I am always under huge pressure during study for my Ph.D. and my pressure come from multiple sources." For example, although participant *A* had worked as a college English teacher for seven years in China before she started her Ph.D., she still had language problems in her doctoral study. Sometimes she could not express herself very well in both writing and classroom discussions. Due to language barriers and cultural differences, she also felt very anxious to communicate with her professors in and outside classrooms.

Similarly, participant *C*, who was a male Ph.D. student studying mathematics in his fifth year, experienced high levels of academic anxiety at the beginning of his doctoral program. He commented that "Of course I experienced a lot of pressure and anxiety. I think [that] the biggest problem [was] is English. [As a teaching assistant,] I had to teach in English. [Further,] I had problem about my study too. Sometimes I could not meet my professors' expectations at the beginning of my program." He further stated that "during the first year of my [doctoral] study, I felt very nervous about my English abilities and doing presentations; but with time, these anxieties faded."

Unlike participants *A* and *C*, participants *B* and *D* reported that they were not experiencing high levels of anxiety in their academic study. Participant *B*, who was a female Ph.D. student studying biology and chemistry, reported that "I do not have much difficulty in my [doctoral] study. I think that it is easier to do a Ph.D. here in America than in China. ... I feel more comfortable and relaxed here [in America]." Similarly, participant D, who was a female Ph.D. student studying organic chemistry, reported that "I do not feel anxious about communicating with professors and classmates. I do not feel anxious about giving presentations either because I had prior teaching experience in China. However, due to the complexity of the content, I do have some nervousness and anxiety about my school work. ... But the anxiety makes me stronger and pushes me to get improvement."

What Factors Contribute to Participants *A* and *D*'s High Levels of Academic Anxiety?

Apparently, both participants *A* and *C* experienced high levels of anxiety in their academic learning. Participant *A* had experienced high level of academic anxiety during her entire doctoral program, whereas participant *C* had experienced high level of academic anxiety in his first year of Ph.D. program. Although participant *C* experienced challenges such as unfamiliarity with North American culture and being far away from family and friends like other CESL students at North American universities, these challenges did not create high level of academic anxiety in his entire doctoral program because he was holding a full-scholarship and did not have any financial burdens. As mentioned above, the major source of his high level of academic anxiety in his first year was inadequate English proficiency. Due to his limited English proficiency, he experienced great anxiety in both his study as a student and teaching as a teaching assistant. But with time and more practice in using English and exposure to English-speaking environment, his high level of academic anxiety was reduced.

However, participant *A*'s situation was very different. As mentioned previously, her high level of academic anxiety comes from multiple sources. First, she was not as lucky as other participants who had received full scholarships to cover both tuition fees and living expenses for their entire Ph.D. programs. Participant *A* just received partial scholarships which covered tuition fees for up to four years. She experienced considerable financial difficulties and reported that "the financial burden and the pressure of keeping my scholarship became a major factor that caused my high level of academic anxiety." Second, language barriers increased her level of academic anxiety. She felt anxious about communicating with professors and peers. She also felt anxious about giving oral presentations and participating in oral discussions, which are generally practiced and encouraged in North American classrooms. Third, cultural differences also added to her academic anxiety. Cultural differences between China and North America created challenges for her to understand academic lectures, meet academic expectations, and interact with North Americans. Fourth, being away from family members and friends caused her loneness and anxiety, which ultimately negatively affect her study. Last but not least, pressure of finding a job directly increased her level of academic anxiety. As an education major Ph.D. student, participant *A* realized the difficulty in finding an employment. She commented that "most education major Ph.D. student find jobs at colleges and universities; however, there are usually dozens of applicants compete for one position. Being a non-English speaker, I am not confident in competing with North Americans."

What Impact Does Academic Anxiety Have on Their Learning?

As commented by participants *A* and *C*, a high level of academic anxiety can negatively affect their learning at North American universities in the following four ways. First, it decreases their self-confidence. Participant *A* commented that "lack of self-confidence can be detrimental to our academic success at North American universities." Second, it lowers their academic performance. "High levels of academic anxiety directly affect our academic achievement. For example, test anxiety can lower our marks," responded by participant *C*. Third, it negatively their social life at the school. For example, being academically anxious can prevent them from socializing and interacting effectively with people on campus. Finally, it leads to negative personal feelings. Participant *A* stated that "I am not happy due to the financial burden of the school; I then become more and more anxious; and more anxiety brings me an even worse mood; and finally I become helpless and hopeless."

What Strategies Have They Developed to Cope with Academic Anxiety?

Participants *A* and *C* have developed effective strategies to cope with their high levels of academic anxiety. Financial burden has created participant *A* tremendous amount of anxiety. She tried to manage money efficiently by "cutting her budget and getting more student loans." Language as a factor has caused both participants *A* and *C* academic anxiety. Participant *A*'s strategy to cope with language barriers was to "talk to professors more" and ask for assistance whenever she needed. Participant *C* believed that he improved his English skills by talking to friends and peers in English and "getting practice as much as possible." Additionally, they also commented that they tried to familiarize themselves with North American classroom culture, develop new study skills, and expand their social network by making more friends and participating in more social activities.

At the same time, they made suggestions for their North American professors. Participant *C* suggested that professors "speak slowly class, and give more chance for students to communicate with them, preferably in person." Similarly, participant *A* commented that professors should "talk to their international students regularly and understand their learning difficulties and needs."

DISCUSSION OF RESULTS

To further examine all interviews with four CESL Ph.D. students studying at these two North American universities, the following observations or conclusions are made. First of all, not all of them are experiencing high levels of academic anxiety.

Participants *A*, who was a social science Ph.D. student, experienced a high level of academic anxiety during her entire program. The other three participants, who are science Ph.D. students were not experiencing high levels of academic anxiety at all with the exception that participant *A* had experienced a high level of academic anxiety in his first year of doctoral study. This finding seems in conformity with previous literature (Huang and Klinger, 2006; Huang and Rinaldo, 2009).

This finding further indicates that the major CESL graduate students are studying for becomes a decisive factor that causes them both challenges and academic anxiety at North American universities. Studies in social sciences (e.g., education, religion) require more language skills and cultural knowledge, whereas studies in mathematics, biology, and chemistry have less linguistic and cultural requirements (Huang, 2006, 2009; Huang and Klinger, 2006). The following comment made by participant *C* provides similar evidence, "math is about special symbol and signals, so there is no trouble to understand each other in class." Therefore, majors that involve more language usage, such as education, political studies, and religious studies, seem to cause greater levels of academic anxiety than those majors that rely more on graphs, tables, numbers and symbols, such as mathematics, biology, and chemistry.

Furthermore, it is apparent that CESL students should be prepared mentally, emotionally and physically before enrolling in a North American university for graduate studies. As suggested by all four participants, one the one hand, prospective students should be aware of these issues and problems they may face during their graduate studies and do whatever they can to prepare themselves; on the other hand, before they leave China they should understand and learn more about the differences between China and North America by taking a course or workshop, which would be a great stepping block into the North American culture.

CONCLUSION

To conclude, this study[1] has provided substantial and detailed information on the understanding of what contributes to CESL graduate students' academic anxiety and how academic anxiety affects their learning at North American universities.

The results are very useful and valuable for both North American educators and CESL students. However, due to the limited number of interviewees (i.e., four CESL students who are all Ph.D. level students), it is suggested that this study be replicated at more North American universities with CESL graduate students at both master's and doctoral levels) to validate the findings. A slight variation might include interviewing some North American professors who teach and/or supervise CESL graduate students.

REFERENCES

Bennett, S. (1999). *Comprehensive multicultural education: Theory and practice.* Allyn and Bacon, Boston, MA.

Canadian Bureau for International Education. (2009). Retrieved October 28, 2009 from the World Wide Web: *http://www.cbie.ca.*

Chen, C. P. (1999). Common stressors among international college students: Research and counseling implications. *Journal of College Conseling, 2,* 49-65.

Clark, C. E., and Schwartz, B. N. (1989). Accounting anxiety: An experiment to determine the effects of an intervention on anxiety levels and achievement of introductory accounting students. *Journal of Accounting education, 7,* 149-169.

Confucius. (1947). The wisdom of Confucius. In S. Commins and R. N. Linscott (Eds.), *Man and man: The social philosophers* (323-358). New York: Random House.

Feng, J. H. (1991). *The adaptation of students from the People's Republic of China to an American academic culture.* Retrieved from ERIC database.

Garcia, C. L. (1998). *Too scared to learn: Overcoming academic anxiety.* California: Corwin Press.

Gay, L. R., and Airasian, P. (2003). *Educational research: Competencies for analysis and applications.* Prentice Hall: New Jersey.

Head, L. Q, and Knight, C. B. (1988). The effects of trait anxiety on state anxiety and perception of test difficulty for undergraduates administered high and low difficulty tests. Paper presented at the Annual Meeting of the Mid-South Educational Research Association, Louisville, KY.

Huang, J. (2009). What happens when two cultures meet in the classroom? *Journal of Instructional Psychology, 36*(4), 335-342.

Huang, J., and Brown, K. (2009). Cultural factors affecting Chinese ESL students' academic learning. *Education, 129*(4), 643-653.

Huang, J., and Rinaldo, V. (2009). Factors affecting Chinese graduate students' cross-cultural learning at North American universities. *International Journal of Applied Educational Studies, 4*(1), 1-13.

---

[1] This article was originally published in *International Journal of Business and Social Science.*

Huang, J., and Klinger, D. (2006). Chinese graduate students at North American universities: Learning challenges and coping strategies. *The Canadian and International Education Journal, 35*(2), 48-61.

Huang, J. (2006). English abilities for academic listening: How confident are Chinese students? *College Student Journal, 40*(1), 218-226.

Huang, J. (2005). Challenges of academic listening in English: Reports by Chinese students. *College Student Journal, 39*(3), 553-569.

Huang, J. (2004). Voices from Chinese students: Professors' use of English affects academic listening. *College Student Journal, 38*(2), 212-223.

Huang, J. (1998). *Students' learning disabilities in a second language speaking classroom.* Paper represented at the Annual Meeting of the American Educational Research Association, San Diego, CA.

Institute of International Education. (2010). *Open Doors Online.* Retrieved July 21, 2010 from the World Wide Web: http://www.opendoors. iienetwork.org.

Lin. L. (2002). *The learning experiences of Chinese graduate students in American social science programs.* Paper presented at the Annual Conference of the Comparative and International Education Society. Orlando, FL.

Liu, D. L. (1994). *Deep sociocultural transfer and its effect on second language speakers' communication.* Paper presented at the annual meeting of the Teachers of English to Speakers of Other Languages, Baltimore, MD.

Myles, J., Quian, J., and Chen , L. (2002). International and new immigrant students' adaptations to the social and cultural life at a Canadian university. *Connections and Complexities: The Internationalization of Canadian Higher Education,* Occasional Papers in Higher Education, Vol. 11, Winnipeg, Center for Research and Development in Higher Education.

Spielberger, C. D. (1983). *Manual for the State-Trait Anxiety Inventory.* Palo Alto, CA: Consulting Psychologists Press.

Sun, W., and Chen, G. M. (1997). *Dimensions of difficulties Mainland Chinese students encounter in the United States.* Paper presented at eh 6th International Conference in Cross-Cultural Communication, Tempe, AZ.

Tweed, R. G., and Lahman, D. R. (2002). Learning considered with a cultural context. *American Psychologist, 57*(2), 89-99.

Upton, T. A. (1989). Chinese students, American universities, and cultural confrontation. *MinneTESOL Journal, 7,* 9-28.

Wan, G. F. (2001). The learning experience of Chinese students in American universities: A cross-cultural perspective. *College Student Journal, 35,* 28-44.

Zhong, M. (1996). *Chinese students and scholars in the U.S.: An intercultural adaptation process.* Paper presented at the 82nd Annual Meeting of the Speech Communication Association, San Diego, CA.

In: East Meets West
Editor: Jinyan Huang

ISBN: 978-1-62618-195-3
© 2013 Nova Science Publishers, Inc.

Chapter 3

CONFIDENCE LEVELS OF CHINESE ESL STUDENTS' ENGLISH ABILITIES

Jinyan Huang[1], and Shuangli Su[2]*

[1]Niagara University, Lewiston, New York, US
[2]Untested Ideas Research Center, Niagara Falls, New York, US

ABSTRACT

Research with ESL students studying at North American universities has indicated that Chinese ESL (CESL) students have difficulties in understanding academic lectures, taking notes, writing assignments, and giving presentations although they have obtained high TOEFL scores. This chapter reports a proportion of a study that investigates their English academic listening challenges as reported by seventy-eight CESL students at an American university. Specifically, this chapter focuses on CESL students' reported confidence in their English abilities for academic listening. Their self-ratings show that reading ability and grammar are the strongest areas, and listening and speaking are the weakest areas. Ninety-two percent of the participants reported having difficulties in understanding English academic lectures. Arts students who had been studying at this American university for less than one year reported that they could only understand sixty to seventy percent of the lectures in their majors.

INTRODCUTION

Research with ESL students studying at North American universities has indicated that Chinese ESL (CESL) students experience considerable challenges in their academic learning: their unfamiliarity with the North American educational culture; their lack of North American academic background; their financial difficulties; their lack of academic study skills and inadequate English proficiency (Chen, 1985; Chen, 1999; Feng, 1991; Liu, 1994; Sun and Chen, 1997; Myles, Qian, and Cheng, 2002; Zhong, 1996). Their lack of English language

---

* Correspondence concerning this chapter should be addressed to Dr. Jinyan Huang at *jhuang@niagara.edu*.

proficiency has become a major challenge in their academic studies. They have difficulties in understanding academic lectures, taking notes, writing assignments, and giving presentations (Huang, 2004, 2005; Yuan, 1982). Their lack of English proficiency was also identified as the biggest obstacle in the process of CESL students' acculturation in the academic context although they came to North American universities with high TOEFL (Test of English as a Foreign Language) and GRE (Graduate Record Examination) scores (Sun and Chen, 1997).

Empirical studies have demonstrated that CESL students have great difficulty in their academic studies at North American universities due to their inadequate English proficiency (Huang, 2004, 2005; Sun and Chen, 1997; Yuan, 1982). However, little research has investigated CESL students' confidence in their English language abilities for academic studies. Through the investigation of their English academic listening challenges, this study also examined their confidence in English abilities for academic listening as reported by CESL students at an American university.

ABOUT THIS STUDY

Seventy-eight CESL students who enrolled in the 2000 winter semester at an American university participated in this study. Table 3.1 shows the demographic information of the participants.

Of the 78 students, 40 (51%) were male and 38 (49%) were female. The females and males were distributed almost equally. Among the 78 participants 36 (46%) were students of arts, and 42 (54%) were science students. The number of arts students and the number of science students were also approximately equal. The students from the following majors were classified as arts students: Linguistics, Education, Law, MBA, and International Studies.

Table 3.1. Result of Demographic Information

Category	Response	Number	Response	Number
Gender	Male	40	Female	38
Major	Arts	36	Science	42
Status	Undergraduates	18	Graduate	60
Length of Time Studying in U.S.	Less than one year	22	More than one year	56
TOEFL Scores	Between 550 and 600	30	Greater than 600	48
Native Language	Mandarin	70	Cantonese	8

The students from the following majors were classified as science students: Computer Science, Mathematics, Chemistry, Accounting, Electrical Engineering, and Biology. Of the 78 students, only 18 (23%) were undergraduate students and 60 (77%) were graduate students. Twenty-two (28%) of them had studied at this American university for less than one year and 56 (72%) for more than one year. All of the 78 participants had achieved a TOEFL score greater than 550 before they came to America, which is the minimum requirement for most of the graduate schools in America, and 48 of them had a TOEFL score greater than 600. All the 78 participants spoke Mandarin Chinese. Seventy of them (90%) spoke Mandarin natively and 8 (10%) spoke Cantonese natively.

A questionnaire was used as the instrument of the study. It consisted of 30 items and an open-ended question. Most of the items required the participants to mark their responses on a five-point Likert scale. The data obtained for the five-point scale items were first analyzed by using descriptive statistical methods. A Factorial ANOVA was then used to determine whether there was a significant difference in the responses according to the following 4 independent variables: a) gender (male/female), b) major (arts/science), c) level of study (undergraduate/graduate), and d) length of time studying in America (less than one year/more than one year). If there were significant differences between the independent variables, a descriptive *post hoc* analysis was conducted to see where the differences occurred.

RESULTS AND DISCUSSION

This chapter focuses on their confidence in English abilities for academic listening as reported by CESL students. It must be pointed out that self-report data are not equal to actual, measured and observed data. Therefore, their self-ratings may not represent CESL students' real English proficiency. The question read as follows: "How confident are you in your English ability for academic listening (pronunciation, grammar, vocabulary, listening, speaking, reading, and writing)? (1 = not at all, 5 = very much)"

The results are summarized in Tables 3.2 and 3.3 Table 3.2 is a summary of CESL students' responses and percents selecting each scale point. In order to emphasize the most frequently selected response in each category, the researcher puts it in bold face in the table. Table 3.3 is a summary of CESL students' reported confidence in their English abilities.

In CESL students' responses, reading ability and grammar are the strongest areas (the mean scores are 3.94 and 3.89 respectively). In fact, no student marked scale point 1 on either of these two items. Only 3.8% of the 78 participants marked scale point 2 on the item that asked about their grammar, and 1.3% marked 2 points on reading. Listening and speaking, however, are their weakest areas according to CESL students' self-ratings. The mean scores were 3.39 and 3.24 respectively. Interestingly, the mean scores of their strong areas are not so different from their weak areas. Their reported mean scores for all the seven language components are between 3.24 and 3.94. This is also in conformity with their reported TOEFL scores. Most participants reported they had achieved very high scores on the TOEFL before they came to study in America.

Table 3.2. CESL Students' Responses and Percents Selecting Each Scale Point

	1	2	3	4	5	N
Pronunciation	0	5.1	**52.6**	32.1	10.2	78
Grammar	0	3.8	23.1	**52.6**	20.5	78
Vocabulary	0	7.7	29.5	**52.6**	10.2	78
Listening	0	10.2	**44.9**	39.8	5.1	78
Speaking	2.6	15.4	**42.3**	34.6	5.1	78
Reading	0	1.3	24.4	**53.8**	20.5	78
Writing	1.3	8.9	**46.2**	34.7	8.9	78

Table 3.3. CESL Students' Reported Confidence in English Abilities for Academic Listening

English Abilities	Number of Responses	Mean	Standard Deviation	Significant Differences (p < .05)
Pronunciation	78	3.47	0.75	① ④
Grammar	78	3.89	0.76	③ ④
Vocabulary	78	3.65	0.76	④
Listening	78	3.39	0.74	③ ④
Speaking	78	3.24	0.86	① ④
Reading	78	3.94	0.70	N/A
Writing	78	3.41	0.82	③ ④

Note: ① Gender ② Major ③ Level of study ④ Length of time studying in America.

Pronunciation

The Factorial ANOVA showed statistically significant differences in participants' self-reported ratings for the component of pronunciation between male students and female students ($p < .05$); and between students who had studied in America for less than one year (1- students) and those who had studied in America for more than one year (1+ students) ($p < .05$). There was no significant difference between graduate students and undergraduate students; and between arts students and science students. The results of the *post hoc* analysis showed that female students (mean = 3.71) were more confident than male students (mean = 3.25), and the 1+ students (mean = 3.57) were more confident than the 1- students (mean = 3.23). This was probably because female students were quicker than male students in learning pronunciation, and over time the 1+ students had become more accustomed to American pronunciation than the 1- students.

Grammar

The Factorial ANOVA showed statistically significant differences in participants' self-reported ratings for grammar between undergraduate students and graduate students ($p < .05$); and 1- students and 1+ students ($p < .05$). There was no significant difference between male students and female students; and between arts students and science students. The results of the *post hoc* analysis showed that graduate students (mean = 4.02) were more confident than undergraduate students (mean = 3.61), and the 1+ students (mean = 4.02) were more confident than the 1- students (mean = 3.59). This was probably because graduate students and the 1+ students had more experience with English grammar learning than undergraduate and the 1- students respectively.

Vocabulary

The Factorial ANOVA showed statistically significant differences in participants' self-reported ratings for the component of vocabulary between 1- and 1+ students ($p < .05$). There was no significant difference between groups in the other three independent variables.

The results of the *post hoc* analysis showed that the 1+ students (mean = 3.84) were more confident than the 1- students (mean = 3.14). This is probably because the 1+ students had studied in America for a longer time than the 1- students, and for this reason they had bigger vocabularies than the 1- students did.

Listening

The Factorial ANOVA showed statistically significant differences in participants' self-reported ratings for the component of listening between undergraduate students and graduate students ($p < .05$), and 1- students and 1+ students ($p < .01$). There was no significant difference between male students and female students; and between arts students and science students. The results of the *post hoc* analysis showed that graduate students (mean = 3.57) were more confident than undergraduate students (mean = 2.78), and the 1+ students (3.57) were more confident than the 1- students (2.91). This was probably because graduate students and the 1+ students had more experience with English academic listening than undergraduate and the 1- students respectively.

Speaking

The Factorial ANOVA showed statistically significant differences in participants' self-reported ratings for the component of speaking between male students and female students ($p < .05$); and 1- students and 1+ students ($p < .01$). There was no significant difference between graduate students and undergraduate students; and between arts students and science students. The results of the *post hoc* analysis showed that female students (mean = 3.47) were more confident than male students (mean = 3.03), and the 1+ students (mean = 3.41) were more confident than the 1- students (mean = 2.82). One fact might explain why female CESL students were more confident in English speaking than male CESL students. In China female high school graduates get much higher scores on the college entrance English oral examination than the males, and more females are selected than males to study English by universities every year. The 1+ students had more experience in English speaking environment, and so they were more confident in English speaking than the 1- students.

Reading

Very interestingly, there was no significant difference between these groups of CESL students on their self-reported ratings for the component of reading. All but one participant marked 3 points or more on their reading ability.

Reading received the highest mean score among all the seven language components, indicating that the participants were most confident in their English reading ability. In China, reading comprehension is emphasized in English teaching in most schools (Ma and Huang, 1992). Therefore Chinese students usually have better reading than listening and speaking in English.

Writing

The Factorial ANOVA showed statistically significant differences in participants' self-reported ratings for the component of writing between undergraduate students and graduate students ($p < .05$), and 1- students and 1+ students ($p < .05$).

There was no significant difference between male students and female students; and between arts students and science students. The results of the *post hoc* analysis showed that graduate students (mean = 3.63) were more confident than undergraduate students (mean = 2.83), and the 1+ students (mean = 3.55) were more confident than the 1- students (mean = 3.05). This was probably because graduate students and the 1+ students had more experience with English writing than undergraduate and the 1- students respectively.

Percentage of Class Lecture CESL Students Comprehend

The above results show that CESL students are not very confident in their English abilities for academic listening. But how confident are they in understanding English academic lectures? The following question asked about the percentage of class lecture in their majors CESL students could understand. The question was as follows: "Approximately what percentage of the class lectures in your major do you understand now?

10% 20% 30% 40% 50% 60% 70% 80% 90% 100%"

The results are shown in Table 3.4.

Table 3.4 shows that 52.8% of the participants reported understanding 80% of the lectures in their majors, and 28.2% of them claimed to understand 90% of class lectures. It was amazing that 8.9% reported understanding 70% of their lectures and 2.6% claimed to understand only 60%; and it was even more amazing that all these participants were arts students who had been studying at this American university for less than one year. Table 4 also shows that 92.3% of all the 78 participants had problems in understanding lectures and only 7.7% of the participants reported fully understanding lectures in their majors.

CONCLUSION

Research shows that some difficulties for ESL students in understanding and remembering information from lectures may be due to the lack of English language abilities itself (Brown, 1994; Ur, 1988). This chapter focuses on the discussion of how CESL students are confident in their English language abilities for academic listening at an American university.

Table 3.4. Percentage of Class Lecture CESL Students Comprehend

10%	20%	30%	40%	50%	60%	70%	80%	90%	100%	N
0	0	0	0	0	2.6	8.9	2.6	28.2	7.7	78

The results indicate that CESL students are not very confident in their English abilities. Their self-ratings show that listening, speaking, writing, pronunciation, and vocabulary are their weak areas.

Students who have been in America for more than one year are more confident in their pronunciation, vocabulary, listening, speaking, and writing than those who have studied in America for less than one year, suggesting the longer one studies in America, the more confident he or she is confident in his or her English abilities.

Similarly, graduate students are more confident in listening and writing abilities than undergraduate students, and female students are more confident in pronunciation and speaking than male students. Surprisingly, there is no significant difference in their self-evaluation of English abilities between arts students and science students. Arts students, however, reported experiencing more linguistic challenges in English academic listening than science students (Huang, 2004, 2005).

Their confidence in English abilities naturally affects the amount of class lectures CESL students believe they can understand. According to the results, only 80% of the 78 CESL students reported understanding 80% or more of the class lectures in their majors and a total of 92.3% of the participants reported having challenges in understanding academic lectures.

Therefore, CESL students need to expose themselves to more English speaking environment as soon as they have come to American universities, and improve both their English abilities and academic skills for understanding English lectures.

It must be mentioned again that the results of this study[1] were based on CESL students' self-report data, which might not represent the real situations. In addition, only 78 CESL students participated in this study. Among the 78 participants, there were only 18 undergraduate students and they could not represent undergraduate Chinese students studying at American universities. All these might affect the generalizibility of this study and limit the researcher's interpretations.

REFERENCES

Brown, H. D. (1994). *Teaching by principles.* New Jersey: Prentice Hall Agents.

Chen, C. P. (1999). Common stressors among international college students: Research and counseling implications. *Journal of College Counseling, 2,* 49-65.

Chen, T. H. (1985). *Cultural differences in classrooms: A comparison of Chinese and US schooling.* Unpublished manuscript.

---

[1] This article was originally published in *College Student Journal.*

Feng, J. H. (1991). *The adaptation of students from the People's Republic of China to an American academic culture.* Reports (ERIC Document Reproduction Service No. ED 329 833).

Huang, J. (2004). Voices from Chinese students: Professors' use of English affects academic listening. *College Student Journal, 38(2),* 212-223.

Huang, J. (2005). Challenges of Academic Listening in English: Reports by Chinese Students. *College Student Journal, 39*(3), 553-569.

Liu, D. L. (1994). Deep sociocultural transfer and its effect on second language speakers' communication. *Paper presented at the annual meeting of the Teachers of English to Speakers of Other Languages*, Maltimore, MD.

Ma, Y. C., and Huang, J. (1992). *A practical guide to English teaching methodology.* Changsha: Hunan Normal University Press.

Myles, J., Qian, J., and Cheng, L. (2002) International and new immigrant students' adaptations to the social and cultural life at a Canadian university. In S. Bond and C. Bowry (Eds.) *Connections and Complexities: The Internationalization of Canadian Higher Education,* Occasional Papers in *Higher Education*, Vol, 11, Winnipeg, Center for Research and Development in Higher Education.

Sun, W., and Chen, G. M. (1997). Dimensions of difficulties Mainland Chinese students encounter in the United States. *Paper presented at the 6th International Conference in Cross-Cultural Communication*, Tempe, AZ. (ERIC Document Reproduction Service No. ED 408 635).

Ur, P. (1988). *Teaching listening comprehension.* Cambridge: Cambridge University Press.

Yuan, D. Z. (1982). *Chinese scientists' difficulties in comprehending English science lectures. Unpublished master thesis,* University of California at Los Angles, Los Angles, CA.

Zhong, M. (1996). Chinese students and scholars in the US: An intercultural adaptation process. *Paper presented at the 82nd Annual Meeting of the Speech Communication Association*, San Diego, CA. (ERIC Document Reproduction Service No. ED 406 704)

ISBN: 978-1-62618-195-3
© 2013 Nova Science Publishers, Inc.

Chapter 4

CHINESE ESL STUDENTS' LEARNING CHALLENGES AND COPING STRATEGIES

Jinyan Huang[1,] and Don Klinger[2]*
[1]Niagara University, Lewiston, New York, US
[2]Queen's University, Ontario, Canada

ABSTRACT

The chapter reports the results of a study that investigated four Chinese ESL (CESL) graduate students' perceptions of the challenges they face and the coping strategies they take in their English academic learning at two North American universities. They reported experiencing the following seven major challenges in their academic learning: a) financial difficulties; b) problems in using English for academic purposes; c) frustrations in becoming a permanent resident; d) difficulty in adapting to classroom learning environment; e) lack of critical thinking skills; f) acculturation problems; and g) loneliness and academic anxiety. For each of the seven challenges they have developed corresponding coping strategies.

INTRODUCTION

Data show that Chinese ESL (CESL) students from the Peoples Republic of China (PRC) are the largest single group of ESL students (Institute of International Education, 2001; Canadian Bureau for International Education, 2002).

Further, approximately eighty percent of the CESL students currently studying at North American universities are graduate students. Generally, they have received their undergraduate education in China before starting their graduate programs in North America.

* Correspondence concerning this chapter should be addressed to Dr. Jinyan Huang at *jhuang@niagara.edu*.

The academic learning experience of this group of CESL graduate students has important educational implications for university administrators and educators.

CESL graduate students arrive from a very different educational system and cultural environment. Research with ESL students studying at North American universities has indicated that CESL graduate students experience considerable challenges in their academic studies (e.g., Chen, 1999; Huang, 2004, 2005; Lin, 2002; Liu, 1994; Myles, Qian and Cheng, 2002; Wan, 2001, Zhong, 1996).

These challenges come from many sources: unfamiliarity with the North American educational culture; lack of North American academic background; financial difficulties; lack of academic study skills and inadequate English proficiency. These factors negatively affect the academic study of these CESL graduate students (e.g., Feng, 1991; Huang, 1998; Huang, 2004, 2005; Sun and Chen, 1997; Upton, 1989).

However, given their generally high rate of success in academic studies and contributions to North American society (Johnson, 2001), these students do develop effective coping strategies to meet these challenges (Lin, 2002). Nevertheless, the exact nature of these challenges and the resulting coping strategies have not been closely examined.

Hence the purpose of this study was to investigate CESL graduate students' perceptions of the challenges they face and the resulting coping strategies they use to support their academic learning at North American universities.

The following three questions drove the study: a) what are CESL graduate students' perceptions of the factors contributing to or impeding their English academic learning, b) which English academic learning challenges have been satisfied or remain, and c) what are the corresponding strategies they use to cope with their academic learning challenges?

THEORETICAL FRAMEWORK

Academic learning, as argued by Tweed and Lehman (2002), varies depending on the cultural context. They proposed a Confucian-Socratic framework to analyze the influence of different cultural contexts on academic learning.

Socrates (469-399 BC), a Western exemplar, valued the questioning of both his own and others' beliefs, the evaluation of others' knowledge, self-generated knowledge, and teaching by implanting doubt. Socratic-oriented learning involves "overt and private questioning, expression of personal hypotheses, and a desire for self-directed tasks" (p. 93).

In contrast, Confucius (551-479 BC), an Eastern exemplar, valued effortful and respectful learning, behavioral reform, and pragmatic acquisition of essential knowledge (Tweed and Lehman, 2002). Confucian-oriented learning involves "effort-focused conceptions of learning, pragmatic orientations to learning, and acceptance of behavioral reform as an academic goal" (p. 93).

Confucian philosophy has had a strong impact on Chinese people's viewpoints, ways of thinking, and behaviors. Confucius believed that success was due mainly from hard work rather than ability. He also alleged that "behavior reform is a central goal of education because virtuous behavior can ensure individual success and societal harmony" (Tweed and Lehman, 2002, p. 92).

In respecting and obeying authorities, one demonstrates "the highest expression of the sense of justice" (Confucius, 1947, p. 332). The goal of pragmatic learning of essential knowledge was to enable individuals to competently conduct themselves within civil service jobs. When Chinese students come to North American universities, many bring a Confucian-oriented perspective to their learning, while their professors and peers may have a more Socratic orientation.

Not surprisingly, these graduate students are unfamiliar and even uncomfortable with North American culture and the North American learning environment. These difficulties are exacerbated by financial difficulties and insufficient English proficiency that further reduce these students' ability to participate in academic and social activities (Feng, 1991; Huang and Klinger, 2004).

In particular, poor English proficiency interferes with understanding and was cited as the major reason that Chinese students rated their first-year academic learning as "not enjoyable" (Huang, 1998).

Unfamiliarity with North American Culture and Classrooms

There is a lack of mutual understanding and common interests between CESL students and their North American peers (Feng, 1991; Lin 2002; Wan, 2001). As an example, North Americans often talk about football and baseball. In contrast, CESL students have little knowledge about such popular North American sports.

Hence CESL students often avoid participating in social activities in North America and have difficulties making real North American friends. Liu (1994) discovered that CESL students in an American university transferred their Chinese cultural values and beliefs into the American context when communicating with Americans. This cultural divide can create communication problems. The principal researcher was recently asked by an American professor, likely Socratic-oriented, "Why do my Chinese students always answer 'yes' (in fact sometimes they have not totally understood) when I ask them whether they have understood my assignments or not?" The professor was then told that in the Chinese culture it would be an embarrassment or even a shame for a Confucian-oriented CESL student to admit not understanding a teacher in front of one's peers. A better solution would be to ask classmates after class.

The cultural divide can also be observed in religious beliefs and holiday celebrations. Chinese people are taught not to believe in God, whereas such a belief is an important part of North American culture. CESL students are very concerned about how to deal with religion in North America (Feng, 1991). North Americans will often talk about God in front of CESL students, try to convince them to believe in God, or bring CESL students to local churches for Sunday services.

In terms of holiday celebrations, the popular North American holidays, Christmas, Thanksgiving, Easter, and Halloween, are not recognized in China. Rather the popular Chinese holidays are the Spring Festival, the Dragon Boat Festival, and the Mid-Autumn Festival. The Chinese notion of celebration and festival also illustrate that these holidays are commemorated very differently. CESL students do not feel the same holiday atmosphere during American Holidays and are often in class during Chinese holidays, away from family and friends. Hence Chinese students in North American universities cannot really enjoy any kind of holidays (Feng, 1991).

Cultural differences in the classroom create anxiety and stress and negatively impact achievement. These differences begin with the unfamiliar structure and facilities of American universities (Sun and Chen, 1997) and continue into student attitudes, classroom interactions, and teaching methodology. Upton (1989) indicated that CESL students have a negative reaction toward American students' behaviors in classroom settings. Tardiness, questioning and challenging professors, or making jokes in class are all considered rude and disrespectful in Chinese classrooms. CESL students also struggle with American students' self-centeredness (Chen, 1985). "They come to the classroom as individuals, study whatever subjects they are really interested in, and do not care much what other people think of them. After class, they would never mind what their fellow students are going to do (quoted in Upton, 1989, p. 24)." In contrast, CESL students do care what the teacher and other students think of them. If students cannot correctly answer the teacher's questions in class, they have "lost face" and feel very embarrassed and even ashamed. As a result, they are often afraid of making mistakes.

Differences in instructional styles have become the biggest challenge for CESL students in American universities and CESL students find it hard to adapt to these differences. Chinese classrooms lack the spirit of equality (Fu, 1991).

Teachers are regarded not only as authorities in their field of study but also students' moral mentor. Chinese teachers are very serious and focus on lecturing. In contrast, North American teachers often use humor and varied, informal teaching methods (Upton, 1989). North American teachers usually regard themselves as facilitators of learning rather than authorities of knowledge. They stress student thinking and discussion, encouraging students to be active in classroom discussions and praising critical and daring ideas (Upton, 1989). CESL students are not used to the vast amount of student participation and discussion in North American classrooms because they think too much student participation affects their understanding of the lecture (Huang, 2005). Interestingly, CESL students feel frustrated that their lack of such higher-level thinking skills makes them passive learners in the classroom (Lin, 2002).

Other differences can be observed in the lack of structure of North American lectures. North American teachers rely far less on textbooks, expect students to complete extensive reading, are not afraid to become "sidetracked" into a tangential topic during a lecture, do not write detailed information on the board, and rarely summarize their lectures (Fu, 1991; Huang, 2005; Upton, 1989). These strategies are viewed by CESL students as indicating poor organization and have been identified as a major factor negatively influencing lecture comprehension.

Strategies Used by CESL Students to Cope with Their Learning Challenges

While a number of studies have explored CESL students' learning challenges in North American universities, few have investigated coping strategies (Chen, 1996; Lin, 2002; Wan, 2001). In order to cope with language difficulties, CESL students "take advantage of their knowledge of reading and writing in English to compensate for their insufficiency in aural and oral English." (Wan, 2001, p. 37) Chen (1996) identifies reflective thinking as the most significant strategy to cope with cultural shock.

Most studies with CESL students were conducted in American university contexts and investigated only their cross-cultural learning challenges. Very limited research, however, has been conducted in Canadian university contexts. In addition, little research has compared CESL students' academic learning challenges and coping strategies between American and Canadian university contexts.

METHODOLOGY

This study was qualitative in nature, because obtaining in-depth information about CESL graduate students' academic learning reality was a major consideration. A random purposive sampling strategy was used to select participants because it added credibility to the study (Gay and Airasian, 2003). Working from a pool of 10 potential participants, four CESL graduate students completed semi-structured interviews. Two of the students were from an American university and two of the students were from a Canadian university. These graduate students came from the fields of Teaching English to Speakers of Other Languages (TESOL), Educational Leadership, Education, and Mechanical Engineering. Two of the students were working at the master's level and two were working to complete their Ph.D. Lastly, three of the students were male and one was female.

The interviews were conducted face-to-face with the students at the Canadian university and by telephone with those at the American university. These interviews allowed the students to describe the "reality" of their academic learning experience at these two North American universities, identifying their perceptions of the factors contributing to or impeding their English academic learning, academic learning challenges, and corresponding strategies to cope with these learning challenges. Activity Theory (Jonassen and Rohrer-Murphy, 1999; Tolman, 1999) guided the development of the interview questions and the analyses of interview data. In order to investigate the participants' perceptions of the factors contributing to or impeding their English academic learning, responses were sorted, categorized, and analyzed under the following factors: sociocultural, educational, linguistic, cognitive, affective, and financial (Huang and Klinger, 2004). As for the identification of their academic learning challenges and corresponding coping strategies, a coding and classifying approach was used (Gay and Airasian, 2003). Responses relevant to these questions were grouped together and then categorized and analyzed according to the recurring themes.

RESULTS AND DISCUSSION

The results of the interviews are summarized below. Participants *A* and *B* were CESL graduate students attending the American university. Participants *C* and *D* were in the Canadian university. Six major factors affecting the four CESL graduate students' cross-cultural academic learning in these two North American universities were identified. Both academic learning challenges and coping strategies were investigated. Seven major academic learning challenges were found: a) financial difficulties; b) problems in using English for academic purposes; c) legal frustrations (resident status); d) difficulty in adapting to the classroom learning environment; e) lack of critical thinking skills; f) acculturation problems; and g) emotional difficulties (loneliness and anxiety). For each of the seven challenges the students developed corresponding coping strategies.

Financial Difficulties

Financial difficulties were ranked as one of the top-three factors negatively affecting academic study for these students at both of these North American universities. Insufficient financial support from both universities created great challenges for them to complete their graduate studies. In response, these students found it necessary to find extra work within their academic institutions. This work involved increased research commitments or non-related work, for example, as a translator or a janitor. These students also found it necessary to spend money very cautiously. As stated by participant *A* "I only buy things that I have to buy, but I never buy stuff beyond my budget or financial ability." Participant *D* went further saying "sometimes I have to control my desire for purchasing things." These financial constraints also affected other pursuits as well. As noted by participant *B*, a PH.D student, "We don't have money for traveling. We have never traveled in US." Similarly, as noted by participant *D*, "I don't have more money for recreational activities."

English Language Problems

Along with financial difficulties, these graduate students ranked insufficient English proficiency as one of the top-three factors negatively affecting their academic study. Although each of these students had obtained very high TOEFL scores, they did not feel confident in their English language proficiency. They all reported having difficulties in using English for academic purposes. In particular, speaking and writing skills were considered to be weak. These students found it difficult to participate during class discussions or give oral presentations. The academic writing process was also found to be challenging especially in terms of format and expectations.

The simplest strategy to cope with these demands is best summarized by participant *D*, "we may spend more hours preparing a research project than native Canadians." At the same time, English listening and speaking skills would best be improved by "talking to native Americans whenever it is possible." In terms of improving reading efficiency, established strategies that include "always paying attention to the key words, the titles, the subtitles, the introduction and the summary, the topic sentence, the first paragraph, and the last paragraph" were identified. Given the importance of academic writing, these students identified a variety of coping strategies including reading sample journal articles before writing, understanding North American academic writing formats such as APA, making use of English writing centers on campus, and continual paper revisions.

Legal Frustrations and Permanent Residency

Many CESL graduate students are interested in obtaining permanent residence status in North America believing that, as stated by participant *A*, "America is more developed. People make more money. There is more privacy. The environment is less polluted. People can afford cars. There is more freedom, including freedom of speech." However, the residency process can be extremely difficult, especially after the September 11 attack. For participant A, the legal frustrations in obtaining permanent residency status was the number one factor negatively affecting his graduate study.

For these graduate students, extending their length of stay in North America appears to be the best method to cope with these legal issues. Like many other Confucian-oriented Chinese students, these students combine this with their future plans. Participant *A* slowed his graduate study program and found part time work. Participant *B* recognized that, even with residency, he would have difficulties obtaining employment in his field. Believing that two PH.D degrees would help ensure employment in North America, he has applied and been accepted into another PH.D graduate program to start once he defends his current dissertation. In contrast, participant *C* did not show any interest in obtaining a permanent resident status in Canada believing it would be almost impossible for her to find a job in Canada. Participant *D* has applied for permanent residency in Canada believing that "having a Canadian permanent resident status will help me go anywhere else, for example, US, England, and Europe."

Adapting to the Classroom Learning Environment

The three social science CESL graduate students in the study noted the greatest classroom challenges. Based on their responses, the main differences between the North American and Chinese classroom learning environments can be summarized in three parts. First, the form of class organization was viewed as very different. They stated that Chinese teachers tend to organize a class in a more formal way or in a step-by-step format, whereas, North American teachers prefer a more informal and casual manner in organizing a class. Second, the students' and teachers' roles were found to be different. These graduate students noted a diminished role of the North American professor coupled with an increased role for students. As noted by participant *A*, "the [North American] teacher doesn't play a critical role in the classroom. The students are playing the most important role in the classroom." Participant *B* went further noting that "in China, teachers take the full responsibility in the classrooms, they use the cramming method. The teachers mainly lecture in class. Students are very passive. They just listen to the teacher. The teachers do not encourage students' participation. Here things are quite different. Teachers encourage students to think. Students' participation is highly encouraged here. They are motivated to join in the class discussions." Because of these differences, the graduate students commented that the North American professor is a stimulator, a supporter and a helper, to help students to learn. In contrast, Chinese professors are givers, and students are receivers. In supporting the North American perspective participant B stated that "In Chinese classrooms, teachers talk too much. They do not encourage students to actively learn, but passively accept."

Finally both the teacher and students have different expectations. In Chinese classrooms, students expect their teachers to give detailed explanations about each topic, because "teachers are regarded as the symbols of knowledge, they are authorities" (participant *B*). Teachers expect their students to be attentive listeners. But in North American classrooms, "students are expected to have read all the required materials before they come to the classrooms. The teacher can ask questions according to the materials, and sometimes explain some difficult and important points. The teacher is only an assistant" (participant *A*). Students can expect their teachers to give them opportunities to ask questions, express their ideas, and to discuss and debate these ideas. In response to these challenges, the study participants noted the importance of learning to interact with North American students, forcing themselves to adapt to the North American classroom environment, and spending more preparation time. Participant *A* was fortunate to meet with a North American student who had previous experience with Chinese students. This student involved participant *A* in small group discussions and would continually ask participant *A* to express his questions or ideas. In the absence of peer support, it was the student's responsibility to "take full responsibility of learning; to be an active learner; spend more time before classes preparing; read extensively about a topic; [and] ask questions whenever it is possible in class" (participant *B*). These students also found that traditional strategies also helped them to prepare for the North American classroom learning. Participant *B* stated that "learning strategies I acquired in China are still effective here in America." These included note taking, memorization of basic concepts, pre-class reading, self study, and review. The demands of these expectations are best summarized by participant *D* noting that "in Canada, I have to be active all the time."

Lack of Critical Thinking Skills

Unlike Socratic-oriented North American students, Confucian-oriented Chinese students are taught to respect and obey authorities. In Chinese culture, teachers are regarded as the symbols of knowledge and they are the authorities over students. As a result, Chinese students are not taught to be critical, an essential requirement in the North American context. These graduate students found it difficult to be critical when reviewing journal articles since books and published papers are viewed as sources of authority in the Chinese system.

In order to become more Socratic-oriented, CESL students need to learn critical thinking skills. Yet, even after six years of experience in an American University, participant *B* explained that it was still not easy for him to learn critical thinking skills. He believed that he was beginning to look at things from different perspectives and was finding the courage to challenge his cultural values and concluded "Critical thinking is what I learned from my cross-cultural learning experience in America. I can get benefit from it all my life. Things cannot develop without critical thinking." Reflecting the Chinese notion of pragmatism, participant A identified a "when in Rome" approach, concluding that "I am now a student in an American university. I need to behave and think like an American. I need to consider things with multiple perspectives. I have to criticize other people's ideas or viewpoints in order to survive in this academic culture."

Acculturation Problems

Due to their cultural and linguistic differences, the four CESL graduate students experience acculturation problems in both of these two North American universities. For example, they all found it very hard to make real friends in North America.

Although their North American classmates were very nice to them, they were unable to develop true friendships with them. In addition, financial and language difficulties also prevented these students from participating in social activities. These challenges all function to slow down their acculturation process in North America.

Acculturation problems were addressed using the three W's: 1) forget who you are; 2) remember where you are, and 3) do what other people do. Participant B explained that CESL students should forget that they are from another culture. If they always isolate themselves from North Americans and consider themselves outsiders, they can never get to know North American culture. In terms of making friends, participant C mentioned that CESL students should treat themselves as equally as they treat North Americans and show interest in communicating with them. Participant D added that CESL students should always remember that they are in North America. They need to take an active attitude toward social activities. Participant A further explained that CESL students need to do what other people do in North America. For example, celebrate Thanksgiving and Christmas as North Americans do. If CESL students respect North American culture, North Americans will surely accept Chinese culture.

Emotional Difficulties

Emotionally, the four CESL graduate students identified two major difficulties, loneliness and anxiety. Being far away from their parents and friends, their daily life is full of loneliness. B's description is a good example: "My daily life is very boring. I spend most of my time at school, taking classes, studying in the library, etc." Not surprisingly, feelings of loneliness were more pronounced when the students talked about family or holiday celebrations. Such loneliness was found to increase stress and negatively impact schooling. Participant D identified a common problem explaining that "I feel very lonely and the loneliness of course affects my emotion. When I don't feel emotionally comfortable, I cannot concentrate on my study here." This only further increased the anxiety of the students as they continued to be anxious about finishing class assignments, writing term papers, and doing research.

Community participation was viewed as the best way to address loneliness, including on campus activities, joining organizations (e.g., the Chinese Students and Scholars Association and International Students Association). The students also found that it was important to take the opportunity to seek help. The only direct strategies to deal with anxiety were to adjust learning methods and strategies and be good at time management.

Further Coping Strategies

The graduate students were asked to use their own experience to provide three suggestions for future Chinese students coming to North America for graduate studies. These strategies generally mirrored responses to the challenges above. Nevertheless, the most important strategies focused on early and careful preparation including obtaining English skills, securing financial support, and understanding the cultural differences before coming to North America. The ability to quickly adapt to the North American culture and learning environment was viewed as a key to success.

CONCLUSION

This study investigated both the learning challenges and coping strategies of four CESL graduate students at two North American universities. Although limited in breadth, the methodology provided an in-depth discussion of the views and experiences of these students. Future research in other university settings and other students would help to validate or expand upon the findings of the current study. It would also be valuable to compare the findings of this study to the experiences of North American professors who teach or supervise CESL graduate students. Within this context, the findings of the current study support previous research identifying factors affecting CESL students. Further, the study has served to identify coping strategies used by these graduate students.

Seven major academic learning challenges were identified along with their corresponding coping strategies. Similar to the findings of Feng (1991), financial difficulties remain one of the top challenges for these CESL students. Careful budgeting and cautious spending are important financial management strategies. Similarly, problems using English for academic purposes continue to pose academic challenges. Several coping strategies were identified to help increase English academic listening, speaking, reading, and writing skills. These strategies focused largely on becoming more active in the classroom and doing more preparatory class work. The North American learning environment also continues to be a challenge. This is best viewed in the difference between the Confucian and Socratic philosophies of learning. In beginning to adjust to the North American learning environment, these graduate students seem to now favor the Socratic-oriented North American classroom learning environment. They appreciate the need to investigate alternative perspectives and develop critical thinking skills. Nevertheless, such skills remain a challenge. The "when in Rome" approach was identified as a successful strategy to address such challenges and not surprisingly, it also appeared to help support the acculturation process, forcing the students to adjust to the North American context. In spite of their attempts to acculturate, CESL graduate students continue to express feelings of loneliness and use participation in activities or local associations to help address this challenge. Previously unreported, these graduate students expressed frustration with the challenges they faced as they attempted to obtain permanent residency. It is not known whether this is a result of an increase in the desire of CESL students to remain in North America or if it is due to changing security policies in the wake of September 11. This frustration has led students to find ways to increase the length of their Educational experience or begin to look for other future options.

In spite of the different geographic context and the variety of experience of the students, the results of the study[1] showed no important differences across graduate program and country of study. All participants experienced similar challenges in their academic learning

---

[1] This article was originally published in *Canadian and International Education*.

processes in North America, although some of their coping strategies for certain challenges differed slightly. The results are important for those CESL students who are currently completing or hope to begin their graduate studies within the North American context. The results also have implications for professors who are responsible for these students. It is hoped that the results of this study will not only help students but also professors begin to understand the challenges that CESL students can be expected to face in North American Universities and the coping strategies that can be used to ameliorate these challenges.

REFERENCES

Canadian Bureau for International Education. (2002, April 15). *International student numbers hit record high, but Canada offers dwindling support for African students.* Retrieved October 28, 2002 from the World Wide Web: http://www.cbie.ca/new s/index_ e.cfm?folder=releasesandpage=rel_2002-04-15_e.

Chen, C. P. (1999). Common stressors among international college students: Research and counseling implications. *Journal of College Counseling, 2,* 49-65.

Chen, S. F. (1996). Learning multiculturalism from the experiences of international students: the experience of international students in a teacher training program. *Paper presented at the Annual Meeting of the American Educational Research Association.* New York, NY. (ERIC Document Reproduction Service No. ED 398177).

Chen, T. H. (1985). *Cultural differences in classrooms: A comparison of Chinese and U.S. schooling.* Unpublished manuscript.

Confucius. (1947). The wisdom of Confucius. In S. Commins and R. N. Linscott (Eds.), *Man and man: The social philosophers* (pp. 323-358). New York: Random House.

Feng, J. H. (1991). The adaptation of Students from the People's Republic of China to an American Academic Culture. *Reports* (ERIC Document Reproduction Service No. ED 329833).

Fu, D. L. (1991). A process classroom through the eyes of an outsider. *Language Arts, 68,* 121-123.

Gay, L. R., and Airasian, P. (2003). *Educational research: Competencies for analysis and applications.* New Jersey: Prentice Hall.

Huang, J. (1998). Students' learning difficulties in a second language speaking classroom. *Paper presented at the Annual Meeting of the American Educational Research Association,* San Diego, CA. (ERIC Document Reproduction Service No. ED 420193).

Huang, J. (2004). Voices from Chinese students: Professors' use of English affects academic listening. *College Student Journal, 38(2),* 212-223.

Huang, J. (2005). Challenges of academic listening in English: Reports by Chinese students. *College Student Journal, 39*(3), 553-569.

Huang, J., and Klinger, D. (2004). Factors affecting Chinese graduate students' cross-cultural learning at North American universities. *Paper presented at the Annual Conference of the Comparative and International Education Society of Canada.* Winnipeg, Manitoba.

Institute of International Education. (2001, May 16). *98/99 opendoors on the Web.* [Selections from the book], New York. Retrieved June 15, 2002 from the World Wide Web: http://www.opendoorsweb.org/Lead%20 Stories/international_studs.htm.

Johnson, J. M. (2001). *Human resources contributions to US science and engineering from China.* SRS Issue Brief. (ERIC Document Reproduction Service No. ED 449026).

Jonassen, D., and Rohrer-Murphy, L. (1999). Activity theory as a framework for designing constructivist learning environments. *Educational Technology, Research and Development, 47*, 61-79.

Lin, L. (2002). The learning experiences of Chinese graduate students in American social sciences programs. *Paper presented at the Annual Conference of the Comparative and International Education Society.* Orlando, FL. (ERIC Document Reproduction Service No. ED 474163).

Liu, D. L. (1994). Deep sociocultural transfer and its effect on second language speakers' communication. *Paper presented at the annual meeting of the Teachers of English to Speakers of Other Languages*, Maltimore, MD.

Myles, J., Qian, J., and Cheng, L. (2002) International and new immigrant students' adaptations to the social and cultural life at a Canadian university. In S. Bond and C. Bowry (Eds.) *Connections and Complexities: The Internationalization of Canadian Higher Education*, Occasional Papers in Higher Education, Vol, 11, Winnipeg, Center for Research and Development in Higher Education.

Sun, W., and Chen, G. M. (1997). Dimensions of difficulties Mainland Chinese students encounter in the United States. *Paper presented at the 6th International Conference in Cross-Cultural Communication*, Tempe, AZ. (ERIC Document Reproduction Service No. ED 408635).

Tolman, C. (1999). Society versus context in individual development: Does theory make a difference? In Engestrom, Y, Miettenin, R., and Punamaki, R. (eds.) *Perspectives on Activity Theory*. New York: Cambridge University Press.

Tweed R. G., and Lehman, D. R. (2002). Learning considered within a cultural context. *American Psychologist, 57(2)*, 89-99.

Upton, T. A. (1989). Chinese students, American universities, and cultural confrontation. *MinneTESOL Journal, 7*, 9-28.

Wan, G. F. (2001). The learning experience of Chinese students in American universities: A cross-cultural perspective. *College Student Journal, 35*, 28-44.

Zhong, M. (1996). Chinese students and scholars in the U. S.: An intercultural adaptation process. *Paper presented at the 82nd Annual Meeting of the Speech Communication Association*, San Diego, CA.

PART 2: EAST MEETS WEST

In: East Meets West
Editor: Jinyan Huang

ISBN: 978-1-62618-195-3
© 2013 Nova Science Publishers, Inc.

Chapter 5

THE FACTORS AFFECTING CHINESE ESL STUDENTS' ACADEMIC LEARNING

Jinyan Huang and *Vince Rinaldo*
Niagara University, Lewiston, New York, US

ABSTRACT

This chapter investigated four Chinese ESL (CESL) graduate students' perceptions of the factors contributing to or impeding their English academic learning at two North American universities. They reported that the following six major factors affect their academic learning: a) socio-cultural factors, b) educational factors, c) linguistic factors, d) cognitive factors, e) affective factors, and f) financial factors. Their satisfaction with and concerns about their academic learning at these two universities were also examined.

INTRODUCTION

During the past two decades, there has been a significant growth in the number of ESL students pursuing academic studies at North American universities. Data from both Institute of International Education (IIE) (2001) and Canadian Bureau for International Education (CBIE) (2002) show that Chinese ESL (CESL) students from the People's Republic of China (PRC) are the largest single group among these ESL students, and approximately eighty percent of the Chinese students currently studying at North American universities are graduate students.

CESL graduate students are from a very different educational system and cultural environment. Research with ESL students studying at North American universities has indicated that many factors affect CESL graduate students' academic studies and these factors include: English language proficiency, Chinese language influence, North American educational culture, Chinese educational background, study skills or strategies, financial and

* Correspondence concerning this chapter should be addressed to Dr. Jinyan Huang at *jhuang@niagara.edu*.

emotional issues (Chen, 1999; Feng, 1991; Huang, 1998; Huang, 2004, 2005; Liu, 1994; Sun and Chen, 1997; Upton, 1989; Yuan, 1982; Zhong, 1996). These factors either contribute to or impede their English academic learning (Huang and Klinger, 2006; Lin, 2002). However, the exact nature of these factors and their levels of satisfaction with and concerns about their academic learning at North American universities have not been closely examined. Hence, the purpose of this study was to mirror the reality of CESL graduate students' academic learning at North American universities. The following two questions informed the study: a) what are CESL graduate students' perceptions of the factors contributing to or impeding their English academic learning; and b) what are their satisfaction with and concerns about their academic learning? Activity theory was used to analyze the set of socio-cultural, educational, linguistic, cognitive, affective, and financial factors perceived by CESL graduate students that affect their academic learning (Jonassen and Rohrer-Murphy, 1999; Tolman, 1999).

CONTEXT

CESL graduate students' are motivated towards the completion of a higher academic degree at North American universities within a cross-cultural or intercultural learning activity. The structure of the activity is constrained by cultural factors including conventions and social strata within the specific context (Jonassen and Rohrer-Murphy, 1999; Tolman, 1999). In order to be successful, these students need to use their knowledge and skills (tools), abide by North American culture, and collaborate with North American professors and peers. Activity Theory was used to analyze the factors influencing CESL graduate students' academic learning at North American universities. It enables the researchers to conceptualize the system of these factors. The following figure shows that this system comprises socio-cultural, educational, linguistic, cognitive, affective, and financial factors. All these factors jointly affect CESL graduate students' cross-cultural learning at North American universities.

Chinese tradition and culture have a great influence on the Chinese people today. Confucian philosophy, in particular, has a strong impact on the Chinese people's viewpoint, way of thinking and behaviors. Confucius believed that success was due mainly to hard work rather than ability. He also alleged that "behavior reform is a central goal of education because virtuous behavior can ensure individual success and societal harmony" (Tweed and Lehman, 2002, p. 92). In respecting and obeying authorities, one demonstrates "the highest expression of the sense of justice" (Confucius, 1947, p. 332). The goal of pragmatic learning of essential knowledge was to enable individuals to competently conduct themselves within civil service jobs. Bearing the Chinese traditional ideas in mind, CESL graduate students surely have certain challenges in their academic learning at North American universities where the cultural environment and educational system are totally differtent.

CESL graduate students often feel uncomfortable with the students' behavior at North American classrooms. Upton (1989) indicates that CESL graduate students at American universities have a negative reaction toward American students' behaviors. Students can be late for class. They often ask the teacher questions or make jokes in class. All of these behaviors are considered rude and disrespectful in Chinese classrooms. In North American classrooms students can challenge teachers at any time by interrupting instruction to ask questions, which can make CESL graduate students feel that students do not show any respect for their teachers.

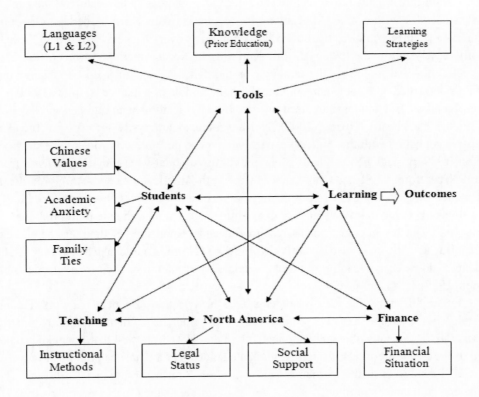

Figure 5.1. A System of Factors Affecting CESL Students' Academic Learning.

The roles of the teachers are defined and interpreted differently in both cultures. Fu (1991) argues that in Chinese culture there is lack of the spirit of equality in the classrooms. Teachers are regarded not only as authorities in their field of study but also as students' moral mentors. While in North American classrooms, there is a fairly equal relationship between teachers and students. Chinese teachers are generally very serious and focus on lecturing but North American teachers often use humor and various informal teaching methods in the classrooms. The difference in teaching style has become the biggest cultural difference for CESL graduate students (Upton, 1989).

North American teachers' different instructional styles or methods affect CESL graduate students' classroom learning. First, in North American classrooms, student participation is encouraged. But most CESL students reported that too much student participation and discussion negatively affected their understanding of academic lectures (Huang, 2005). Second, North American teachers usually regard themselves as students' facilitators of learning but not their authorities of knowledge. They can admit their ignorance on a topic. Generally, they do not easily get angered by students' challenging questions as do Chinese teachers. North American teachers give students' freedom to express their different ideas. They do not directly give answers to particular questions. What they stress is students' thinking and discussion. Therefore, they encourage students to be active in classroom discussions and praise critical and daring ideas (Upton, 1989). Third, North American teachers' poor lecture organization and failure to follow textbooks creates challenges for most CESL students understanding of academic lectures (Huang, 2005). In Chinese culture, teachers carefully organize their lectures and generally summarize the lecture at the end of it. CESL students had the same expectations for lectures in their North American classrooms. Further, in Chinese culture, textbooks have authority over teachers (Fu, 1991). Teachers usually closely follow the textbook while lecturing. In North America, however, teachers do not feel compelled to follow the textbook or the syllabus, and they do not "worry about getting sidetracked onto some tangential topic in the middle of a lecture" (Upton, 1989, p. 25) either. Finally, CESL students are used to point-by-point lectures with outlines and key points put on the blackboard (Huang, 2005). North American university lectures are broad and extensive compared with the "intensive, narrow, and detailed" lectures in Chinese classrooms (Upton, 1989, p.25). CESL students often get confused about what they should learn from a lecture. Therefore, CESL students expect their North American teachers' to give a detailed explanation of every topic and to put the key points or outlines on the blackboard in order for them to take detailed notes. When their expectations are not met, they tend to think that their North American teachers are not as resourceful and responsible as their teachers back in China. But actually it is also a cultural difference. North American teachers expect their students to do extensive reading and look for related information on their own outside of class (Upton, 1989).

Another difficulty that CESL students face is a lack of financial support. Financial difficulty has a strong negative impact on CESL graduate students at North American universities. The results of a study conducted by Feng (1991) showed that financial problems were of the greatest concern for CESL graduate students at a southern American university. Most of the subjects in this particular study suffered from heavy financial pressures. They struggled with money problems, which seriously affected their basic everyday life. How could they concentrate on their academic learning? In order to survive some CESL graduate students had to work after school, doing heavy labor and earning only minimum wages to support living. Financial support in the form of scholarships, fellowships, teaching and research assistantships from the North American universities and the tuition fees as well as other expenses have become the most important criteria for CESL students from PRC when choosing North American graduate schools. Feng (1991) concluded in the study that generally Chinese students' financial situations have a negative impact on their academic achievement, English language skill improvement, as well as their participation in social activities.

Language is also an important factor that affects CESL graduate students' academic learning. Those who have serious initial language problems, have difficulties understanding academic lectures, American idioms and jokes, and in taking notes (Feng, 1991; Huang, 2006). The English language problem was identified as the biggest obstacle in the process of CESL graduate students' intercultural adjustment although they came to the United States with high TOEFL (Test of English as a Foreign Language) and GRE (Graduate Record Examination) scores (Sun and Chen, 1997). The lack of English language proficiency has a strong negative impact on their communication with North Americans academically and socially. In Huang's (1998) study seventeen out of eighteen CESL graduate students rated their first-year academic learning as not "enjoyable" because of their "tremendous" language difficulty in their academic learning.

Cultural differences in the classroom create anxiety and stress and negatively impact learning. These differences begin with the unfamiliar structure and facilities of American universities (Sun and Chen, 1997) and continue into student attitudes, classroom interactions, and teaching methodology. Huang (2005) indicated that 66.8% of the CESL students reported that anxiety negatively affected their understanding of English lectures in American classrooms. Some subjects commented that they became anxious because their American teachers asked so many questions in class.

These studies with CESL graduate students investigated only the negative side of their English academic learning experience in North American universities. This theory-driven study explored both negative and positive aspects to mirror the reality of CESL graduate students' English academic learning experiences at two North American universities.

METHOD

The purpose of this study was to hear the voices of CESL graduate students about both their successful and unsuccessful academic learning experiences at North American universities. Specifically, it was to a) investigate their perceptions of the factors contributing to or impeding their English academic learning, and b) explore their satisfaction with and concerns about English academic learning. Because the purpose of this study was to obtain in-depth information about CESL graduate students' academic learning reality, semi-structured interviews were conducted. A random purposive sampling strategy was used to select participants because it added credibility to the study (Gay and Airasian, 2003). A sample of four CESL graduate students, two from an American university (participants *A* and *B*) and two from a Canadian university (participants *C* and *D*) participated in the study. Semi-structured interviews were conducted between the principal researcher and the participants to mirror the reality of their academic learning experience at these two North American universities.

At the time of the interview participant *A* was a Masters of Arts (MA) student majoring in Teaching English to Speakers of Other Languages (TESOL). He came to the American university to study for his MA in August 1998. He was in his fifth year of study and was preparing to graduate shortly.

Participant *B* was a Ph.D. student majoring in Educational Leadership. He came to the same American university in August 1998, and started his Master's program in September. He got his MA in 2000 and then continued to work on his PhD program in the same area. He is in his final year of his doctoral program.

Participant *C* was a Master's student majoring in Education. She had started her graduate program at a Canadian university approximately two months before the interview.

Lastly, participant *D* was a Ph.D. student majoring in Mechanical Engineering. He started his Ph.D. program at the same Canadian university in May 2002.

The interviews were conducted face-to-face with the students at the Canadian university and via telephone with those at the American university. These interviews allowed the participants to describe the "reality" of their academic learning experience at these two North American universities, identifying their perceptions of the factors contributing to or impeding their English academic learning, and their satisfaction with and concerns about English academic learning. Activity Theory (Jonassen and Rohrer-Murphy, 1999; Tolman, 1999) guided the development of the interview questions and the analyses of interview data. In order to investigate the participants' perceptions of the factors contributing to or impeding their English academic learning, their responses were sorted, categorized, and analyzed under the following factors: socio-cultural, educational, linguistic, cognitive, affective, and financial factors (Huang and Klinger, 2006). As for the identification of their satisfaction with and concerns about English academic learning, a coding and classifying approach was used (Gay and Airasian, 2003). Responses relevant to these questions are grouped together and then categorized and analyzed according to the recurring themes.

RESULTS AND DISCUSSION

From the interviews there emerged six major factors that affected these four CESL graduate students' cross-cultural academic learning at the two North American universities. These factors were identified as a) socio-cultural factors, b) educational factors, c) linguistic factors, d) cognitive factors, e) affective factors, and f) financial factors. Further, the top-three positive and top-three negative factors were further explored as were both their satisfaction with and concerns about their academic learning.

Socio-cultural Factors

All four participants agreed that due to the social and cultural differences between China and North America several factors both helped and impeded their academic learning. One significant area was the role played by family. As was stated by participant *B* whose parents are both professors at a Chinese university, *"Family, as a factor, can help but also impede my graduate study"*. The participant's parents have been teaching in the university since they graduated in the 1960s and both hold very high expectations for their son. It is important to note that although participant *B* was married before he came to America to begin his graduate study; his wife did not come to America until after his sixth month of study. He made the following comments:

"Family as a factor, I think, helps my graduate study. I could still remember the first six months I spent in America alone. I got married several years ago, before I came to study in [the] U.S. This was the first time we separated from each other. I felt very lonely at first. I missed my family when I was in [the] U.S. After six months my wife came to [the] U.S., which helped my study a lot. Her coming to [the] U.S. was a very positive event for my study. If my wife had not come to [the] U.S., I might have changed my study plan. I would have ended my study here and gone back to China."

It is apparent that although family plays a positive role in driving the student to achieve, the longing for absent spouses and parents can have a negative emotional impact which ultimately has a negative impact on student academic achievement. This sentiment was reiterated by Participant *D* whose father is a university professor in China and whose mother is a retired accountant. Participant *D* was married just before he came to study in Canada. His wife, who works in a big city, has remained in China. In this case, family was found to negatively affect his study in Canada.

"Of course family as a factor has an effect on my study, generally this effect is negative. I always miss my family members in China. I can feel very sad, especially on occasions of holidays. I feel very lonely and the loneliness of course affects my emotion. When I don't feel emotionally comfortable, I cannot concentrate on my study here."

The feelings for family are further compounded by residency issues and the need for visas. Maintaining a legal status in America is a very important rule for international students, especially after September 11, 2001. Because many CESL graduate students in social sciences choose research topics that have a Chinese context, they need to go back to China regularly to attend conferences and collect data. However, because of the strict immigration laws, these students have to re-apply for a U.S. visa each time in order to re-enter America and many CESL graduate students have been declined re-admittance. This has a profoundly negative influence on them as well as others seeking to complete American degrees. This pressure coupled with the pressure of having to report to the immigration office their new addresses while residing in America further exacerbates their feelings of anxiety.

"I have studied in America for 5 years without going back to China. My parents are in China and I feel so sorry about being away from them for such a long time. I did not go back to China to visit my parents because I know it's hard for me to get a U.S. visa to come back to America." (Participant *A*)

Both participants *A* and *B* expressed an interest in obtaining an American permanent resident status after finishing their graduate programs in America. In order to obtain a permanent resident status, however, they will need to first find employment in America which is very difficult. Both participants *A* and *B* expressed their own concerns about becoming permanent residents in America.

"Actually I should have graduated two or three years ago. I did not choose to graduate two or three years ago because I was afraid that I could not find a job in America. If I could not find a job I had to go back to China. I prefer staying in America for several reasons. America is more developed than China. People also make more money here. There is more privacy in America than in China. The environment is less polluted. People can afford cars. There is more freedom, including freedom of speech." (Participant *A*)

"My ultimate goal is to go back to China for my personal development. But before I go back to China, I need some working experience in America. Therefore, I want to work in America for some years after I have finished my degree. A job in America, plus a legal status, can be a pleasant thing. Why not stay?" (Participant *B*)

Participants *C* and *D* were studying at the Canadian university and voiced similar concerns to the participants studying at the American university:

"Yes, maintaining a legal status in Canada negatively affects my study here. My visa was only valid for one year, but my program is a 3 and [a] half year program. It does not make any sense. I got very frustrated to renew my visa. There is another thing that can cause problems, that's [the] study permit for an international student. It takes [a] very long time to get it. Also the process of applying for a visa takes [a] long time. It can sometimes affect my home visit plan and finally affect my study here."

However, unlike her American counterpart, participant *C* did not show any interest in obtaining a permanent resident status in Canada. She did not want to become a Canadian permanent resident because it was almost impossible for her to find a job in Canada.

Although participant D had submitted his Canadian permanent resident application, he expressed a very unique consideration:

"Yes, I want to be permanent resident in Canada. I have already submitted my application. Staying in Canada is good for my personal development. I may not permanently live in Canada. But having a Canadian permanent resident status will help me go anywhere else, for example, [the] U.S., England, and Europe. Therefore, my intention of applying for a Canadian permanent resident status is only a temporary consideration."

The need to connect with family is one that is heightened by an inability or awkwardness in establishing new friendships while in North America. All of the participants found it very hard to make friends in North America. Participant *A* had attempted to make a few American friends, but his friends were not students. Participant *B* mentioned that *"because of our different linguistic and cultural backgrounds, and values, it is hard for us international students to make many American friends."* Participants *C* and *D* likewise provided similar comments.

"I find it difficult to make friends here. It is because of cultural difference. The Canadian students, I mean my classmates are very nice. But we don't talk very much. I guess maybe it's because we don't know what to talk [about]. It's very hard to find common topics for communication because our backgrounds are very different." (Participant *C*)

"I prefer making friends with Chinese people in Canada. I think it's hard to make Canadian friends. The main reason is the cultural difference; different ways of thinking, and different values. I have attempted to make friends with native Canadians, but did not make any." (Participant *D*)

Socially, all four participants commented that most people were very helpful in their neighborhood and they were happy to help them if they did need help; however, only the students studying at the doctoral level believed that they received sufficient help from their supervisors, instructors and other professors in their academic departments.

Educational Factors

The four participants completed their undergraduate education in China. Participants *A*, *C*, and *D* also received their Master's degrees from Chinese universities. And according to each, their prior education in China had a strong effect on their academic learning in North America.

The four participants strongly agreed that their educational experience in China helped their study in North America. For example, participants *A*, *B*, and *D* had English as their undergraduate major. They indicated that their English learning experience was helpful for their academic learning. Participant *C*, who had an undergraduate major in computer science, made the following comments:

"I have had a very good foundation of using computer applications in China. For example, programming and hardware are my advantages. Also I have a strong mathematical foundation. Both my computer and mathematics knowledge can greatly help my study here."

All the participants commented that there was a huge difference between Chinese and North American classroom teaching styles and their classroom learning experience in China had a strong negative impact on their classroom learning in North America. They agreed that the teacher did not teach much in a North American classroom; most class time was spent on discussion and group work; the students were playing a very important role in the classroom. While in a Chinese classroom, things were just the opposite. Participant *B* made the following comments:

"When I first came here, I was not used to the classroom teaching. The classroom teaching here was very different from the situation in China. In China, teachers take the full responsibility in the classrooms. They use the cramming method. The teachers mainly lecture in class. Students are just passive listeners. The teachers do not encourage students' participation. Here things are quite different. Teachers encourage students to think. Students' participation is highly encouraged here. They are motivated to join in the class discussions. So we Chinese students feel difficult to be a member of the classroom discussions. As a result we feel very disappointed. This can also be part of cultural shock. ... The role of the teacher in American classrooms, I think, is a helper, to help students to learn. Students are the centre of the classroom. Students are supposed to have read all the required materials before they come to the classrooms. The teacher can ask questions according to the materials, and sometimes explain some difficult and important points. The teacher is only an assistant. This is the big difference between an American classroom and a Chinese classroom."

Linguistic Factors

As expressed by the four participants, both Chinese (L1) and English (L2) had an effect on their academic learning at these two North American universities. The effect could be both positive and negative. It is well-known that L1 produces both positive and negative transfers for L2 learners (Ellis, 1994). Chinese, therefore, can both help and impede CESL graduate students' English academic learning. The impact of Chinese on their graduate study could be reflected in the comments made by participants *C* and *D*, each of whom believed that the structure of their mother tongue assisted them in organizing ideas in English. Although the four CESL graduate students had scored very high on TOEFL, a required English test for non-native speakers of English who want to pursue academic studies at English-speaking universities, they were not very confident in their English language proficiency. They all agreed that their insufficient English proficiency negatively affected both their academic and social activities. Although comfortable with their English proficiency while in China, the participants often found it uncomfortable to express themselves either socially or in class.

Cognitive Factors

All the four participants responded that they needed more critical and creative thinking skills, but they believed they could learn to take effective learning approaches or strategies when they were facing a different learning culture. They agreed that they were active and successful learners at these North American universities.

One of the fundamental social differences that exist between the two schools of education is the role of the learner. In Chinese culture, students are taught not to challenge authority. Teachers are regarded as the symbols of knowledge and they are the authorities over students (Fu, 1991). As a result, Chinese students do not learn to be critical. But in North American learning context, critical thinking is a requirement. The participants found it hard to be critical. Participant *A* commented that:

"Writing critiques is a basic requirement for a graduate student in American university context. I have problems in criticizing other people's ideas. In Chinese culture, books have authorities over teachers, and teachers have authorities over students. We treat published papers [as] authorities."

Rather than critical thinking, memorization is a popular learning strategy used by Chinese students. People might argue that this strategy may appear to be surface oriented (Tweed and Lehman, 2002) but if it is used as a path to understanding, it works.

"I think that memorization is important. Basic things, common knowledge should be memorized. Memorization should be based on understanding and also should lead to better understanding. The promotion of abilities, for example, creative ability, writing ability, expressive ability, and research ability for graduate students are more important than just memorizing things." (Participant *B*)

Affective Factors

CESL graduate students coming to study in North America have only been introduced to the beginning of a hard new experience and a long affective torment (Huang and Klinger, 2006). North America is filled with pressures. As told by the participants, loneliness and anxiety were often connected to the absence of family and friends, two major affective factors that negatively affected their graduate study here. Being far away from their parents and friends, the four participants expressed that their daily life in North America was full of pressures and loneliness. Every day they were routinely doing the same things.

"My daily life is very boring. I spend most of my time at school, taking classes, studying in the library, etc. My daily life is also very stressful. Classes, assignments, and examinations can make my daily life full of stresses. In addition, loneliness also negatively affects my study." (Participant *B*)

The participants explained that they were experiencing a high level of academic anxiety which negatively affected their academic study.

"When I first started my graduate program, I was very anxious about finishing my assignments on time. I also worried about writing course papers. In class I was anxious about participating class discussions, and sometimes, being asked to answer questions. In the following years I worried about writing my thesis and defending my thesis. Currently I worry about finding a job. Anxiety, as a factor, has negative impact on my graduate study here." (Participant *A*)

Financial Factors

Financially, the four participants were experiencing difficulties. According to them, insufficient financial support from both universities had created considerable challenges for them in completing their graduate study. Although offered scholarships, the monetary reimbursement did not even cover a term's tuition. Financial pressure has affected not only their basic everyday life but also their academic study (Huang and Klinger, 2006). With insufficient financial support, they could not participate in any social activities. As a result, their acculturation process slowed down.

"Most of my money is from my parents. I got scholarship here, but just a very small amount. It was not enough even to pay a term's tuition. Also I got some savings myself. I worked a few years before I came to Canada to study." (Participant C)

Despite these difficulties, all four participants were generally satisfied with their academic study in North America; however, they did express some concerns. Participant C had studied in Canada for just two months, but she was quite satisfied with her study believing that there were a lot of resources at the university that were available to her and that the professors, the librarians, and the classmates were all very helpful. Participant B who had been in his graduate programs for about six years commented:

"My satisfaction outweighs my concerns. I learned knowledge and skills. But more importantly, I understood American culture and values. I learned how to respect people and respect other peoples' values. Academically, I understood American educational system. I learned many education theories. Meanwhile I gained more educational experiences. I also learned how American people are doing educational research, which can help my own research in the future."

When talking about their concerns, the four participants expressed worries about their future personal development. They want to find employment in North America after they finish their degrees but they were not very confident in their ability to find jobs in the North American market. Although they identified difficulties acculturating to North American society, they believed that they had acculturated to the point that they may find it difficult readapting to the Chinese way of life once they returned home even though at least one of the participants believed that China provided the best opportunities for him.

When asked to identify the top-three factors that had positively affected their North American academic learning experiences, the four participants cited the academic culture that emphasized independence and the non-competitive atmosphere created by their professors and classmates. Two of the four also cited their strong grounding in content which they attributed to their Chinese education. When asked to identify the top-three factors that had negatively affected their North American academic learning experiences the four participants cited issues with residency, a lack of proficiency with the English language and culture, and the lack of financial support.

The last interview question asked of the four participants' dealt with their self-evaluation of cross-cultural learning experiences at these two North American universities. All four found the experience to be very positive, challenging and beneficial to their future careers.

CONCLUSION

Guided by Activity Theory, this study investigated four CESL graduate students' perceptions of the factors that had affected their academic learning at two North American universities. Six major factors that both positively and negatively affected their academic study were identified. First, among socio-cultural factors, maintaining a legal status and obtaining a permanent resident status, making North American friends, and their family ties in China, were factors that had negatively affected their graduate study; the help they had received from the families and social and academic communities had positively affected their academic study. Second, their prior education in China generally had produced a positive impact on their study in North America; but their classroom learning experience in China had produced a negative impact. Third, lack of English proficiency always impeded their study; while Chinese sometimes helped with their writing in English. Fourth, among cognitive factors, lack of critical thinking had produced a negative impact; while memorization as a path to understanding helped their learning. Fifth, such affective factors as loneliness and academic anxiety had produced a negative impact on their academic study. Finally, similar to what Feng (1991) and Huang and Slinger (2006) had found, all participants indicated that they had financial problems and the insufficient financial support always negatively affected their graduate study in North America. The financial factor was identified as one of the top three factors that had negative impact on their study by all four participants.

The results of the study showed no big differences by both graduate program and the country where the university is located. All participants' overall evaluations of their North American cross-cultural learning experience were positive, although they expressed some concerns about their future personal development.

The results are important for those CESL students who are currently completing or hope to begin their graduate studies in North American universities. The results also have implications for North American professors who are responsible for these students. It is suggested that this study be replicated at more North American universities where there are CESL graduate students to validate findings of this study. A slight variation might include interviewing some North American professors who have CESL graduate students in their classes or who supervise CESL graduate students[1].

REFERENCES

Canadian Bureau for International Education. (2002, April 15). *International student numbers hit record high, but Canada offers dwindling support for African students.* Retrieved October 28, 2002 from the World Wide Web: http://www.cbie.ca/ news/index_ e.cfm?folder=releasesandpage= rel_2002-04-15_e

Chen, C. P. (1999). Common stressors among international college students: Research and counseling implications. *Journal of College Conseling, 2,* 49-65.

Confucius. (1947). The wisdom of Confucius. In S. Commins and R. N. Linscott (Eds.), *Man and man: The social philosophers (pp. 323-358).* New York: Random House. (Original work published ca. 479 B. C. E.)

Ellis, R. (1994). *The study of second language acquisition.* Oxford: Oxford University Press.

Feng, J. H. (1991). *The adaptation of Students from the People's Republic of China to an American Academic Culture.* Reports (ERIC Document No. ED 329 833).

Fu, D. L. (1991). A process classroom through the eyes of an outsider. *Language Arts, 68,* 121-123.

Gay, L. R., and Airasian, P. (2003). *Educational research: Competencies for analysis and applications.* Prentice Hall: New Jersey.

---

[1] This article was originally published in *International Journal of Applied Educational Studies.*

Huang, J. (1998). *Students' learning difficulties in a second language speaking classroom.* Paper presented at the Annual Meeting of the American Educational Research Association, San Diego, CA. (ERIC Document Reproduction Service No. ED 420 193)

Huang, J. (2004). Voices from Chinese students: Professors' use of English affects academic listening. *College Student Journal, 38*(2), 212-223.

Huang, J. (2005). Challenges of academic listening in English: Reports by Chinese students. *College Student Journal, 39*(3), 553-569.

Huang, J. (2006). English abilities for academic listening: How confident are Chinese students? *College Student Journal, 40*(1), 218-226.

Huang, J., and Klinger, D. (2006). Chinese graduate students at North American universities: Learning challenges and coping strategies. *The Canadian and International Education Journal, 35*(2), 48-61.

Institute of International Education. (2001, May 16). *98/99 opendoors on the Web.* [Selections from the book], New York. Retrieved June 15, 2002 from the World Wide Web:http://www.opendoorsweb.org/Lead%20 Stories/international_studs.htm

Jonassen, D., and Rohrer-Murphy, L. (1999). Activity theory as a framework for designing constructivist learning environments. *Educational Technology, Research and Development, 47*, 61-79.

Lin, L. (2002). *The learning experiences of Chinese graduate students in American social sciences programs.* Paper presented at the Annual Conference of the Comparative and International Education Society. Orlando, FL. (ERIC Document Reproduction Service No. ED 474 163)

Liu, D.L.(1994). *Deep sociocultural transfer and its effect on second language speakers' communication.* Paper presented at the annual meeting of the Teachers of English to Speakers of Other Languages, Maltimore, MD.

Sun, W. and Chen, G. M. (1997). *Dimensions of difficulties Mainland Chinese students encounter in the United States.* Paper presented at the 6th International Conference in Cross-Cultural Communication, Tempe, AZ. (ERIC Document Reproduction Service No. ED 408 635)

Tolman, C. (1999). Society versus context in individual development: Does theory make a difference? In Engestrom, Y, Miettenin, R., and Punamaki, R. (eds.) *Perspectives on Activity Theory.* NY: Cambridge University Press.

Tweed R. G., and Lehman, D. R. (2002). Learning considered within a cultural context. *American Psychologist, 57*(2), 89-99.

Upton, T. A. (1989). Chinese students, American universities, and cultural confrontation. *Minne TESOL Journal, 7*, 9-28.

Yuan, D. Z. (1982). *Chinese scientists' difficulties in comprehending English science lectures.* Master's thesis, University of California at Los Angles, Los Angles.

Zhong, M. (1996). *Chinese students and scholars in the U. S.: An intercultural adaptation process.* Paper presented at the 82nd Annual Meeting of the Speech Communication Association, San Diego, CA.

In: East Meets West
Editor: Jinyan Huang

ISBN: 978-1-62618-195-3
© 2013 Nova Science Publishers, Inc.

Chapter 6

THE IMPACT OF CULTURAL DIFFERENCES ON CHINESE ESL STUDENTS' ACADEMIC LEARNING

Jinyan Huang and *Kathleen Brown*
Niagara University, Lewiston, New York, US

ABSTRACT

Confucianism meets Constructivism in North American universities and our classrooms are failing to meet the educational expectations of Chinese ESL (CESL) students. Specifically, students from the People's Republic of China mentioned six areas where they feel discomfort: a) they feel uncomfortable with the classroom behavior of North American students; b) they question the value of a professorial focus on discussion rather than lecture; c) they query the professor's failure to follow the textbook; d) they feel there is too much emphasis on group work; e) they note a lack of lecture summaries along with an apparent lack of organization; and f) they share no common interests (e.g. sports, religion) with their North American counterparts. This chapter discusses the cultural factors that affect CESL students' academic learning at North American universities. It also provides implications for North American professors.

INTRODUCTION

ESL students have several challenges in their academic studies at North American universities. Studies have shown that these challenges come from different sources: students' inadequate English proficiency; their unfamiliarity with the North American culture; their lack of appropriate study skills or strategies; their academic learning anxiety; their low social self-efficacy; their financial difficulties; and their separation from family and friends (Althen, 1999; Arthur, 1997; Berman and Cheng, 2001; Bontrager, Birch, and Kracht, 1990; Chen, 1999; Deressa and Beaver, 1988; Ferris and Tagg, 1996; Leung and Berry, 2001; Owie, 1982; Trice, 2001). These studies provide important information not only for North American

---

* Correspondence concerning this chapter should be addressed to Dr. Jinyan Huang at *jhuang@niagara.edu*.

professors, who need to be aware of their ESL students' academic learning difficulties, but also for North American universities, in order that supporting services for ESL students on campus can be improved.

Chinese ESL (CESL) students from the People's Republic of China are the largest single group of ESL students studying at North American universities (Canadian Bureau for International Education, 2002; Institute of International Education, 2001). Approximately eighty percent of the CESL students currently studying at North American universities are graduate students[*]. They generally have received their undergraduate education in China prior to commencing graduate school in North America. The academic learning of CESL students at North American universities has important implications for university administrators and other educators.

CESL students are from a very different cultural environment and educational system. Research has begun to show that CESL students have considerable challenges in their academic studies at North American universities (Chen, 1999; Feng, 1991; Huang, 2004, 2005, 2006; Huang and Klinger, 2006; Liu, 1994; Myles, Qian and Cheng, 2002; Sun and Chen, 1997; Upton, 1989; Zhong, 1996). Students from different cultures learn in different ways, and may differ in their learning styles, self-expressions and communication styles (Bennett, 1999). Chinese culture is very different from the culture of North America. The question of how cultural differences affect CESL students' academic learning at North American universities merits closer examination.

This chapter first examines CESL students' cultural and educational backgrounds. Then it discusses how cultural differences affect their academic learning at North American universities. Finally it provides some implications for North American professors and educators, namely, how they could work with CESL students to minimize academic learning difficulties caused by cultural factors.

CESL Students' Cultural Background

China is a country with a long history and unique culture. Chinese tradition and culture have a great influence on the Chinese people today. Confucian philosophy has a strong impact on the Chinese people's viewpoint, way of thinking and behaviors (He, 1996). One cannot begin to talk about Chinese culture and education without discussing Confucius and his philosophy (Qian, 2002).

Confucius and his followers have largely influenced Chinese society in general and education in particular (Shen, 2001). The influence can also be felt in other Asian countries. Many of the Chinese traditional values rooted deeply in Confucian philosophy still have tremendous impact on Chinese people's life. For example, "filial piety, respect for the elderly, and moderation" (p. 3) are regarded as Chinese virtues.

Confucius emphasized the importance of harmony. Harmony, according to Confucius, is delightful and enduring (He, 1996). In a family, the parents always have authority over their children and the children should respect their parents. In the schools, the teachers are regarded as the authorities. The students should always respect the teachers. In the society the children

---

[*] Throughout this chapter, the term 'CESL students' refer to 'CESL graduate students who are from the People's Republic of China and currently studying at North American universities.'

should always show respect for the older people; persons of lower social status should be loyal to the authorities. All these became the Chinese moral standard.

Confucius is regarded as one of the fifty major thinkers on education (Palmer, 2001). His influence on education can be summarized as the following three major points (Shen, 2001): First, his principle that "Those who excel in office should learn; those who excel in learning should take office" has guided Chinese education. The principle provided justifications for the imperial examinations, which selected officials according to one's merits. This system was abandoned in the year 1905. Confucius thought that education should be available to everybody regardless of their social status.

Second, a large body of literature produced at the Confucius private school became the teaching materials in Chinese schools for centuries until the year 1905. "The Five Classics" and "The Four Books", for example, were the basic texts for the imperial examination. Confucius focused on classics and completely ignored practical and scientific knowledge.

Third, the Confucian philosophy of education stressed the social rather than individual development. He advocated the moral values that were actually related to governing social relationships. He asked his students to "achieve self-cultivation first, and then family harmony, later on good order in the state, and finally peace in the empire" (Shen, 2001, p. 4). The fundamental principle of Confucian education was to train talent loyal to the government. This is still true in current Chinese education.

Confucius' philosophy on learning can be summarized as follows (Tweed and Lehman, 2002): "effortful learning, behavioral reform, pragmatic learning, acquisition of essential knowledge, and respectful learning" (p. 91). Confucius stressed the importance of hard work. He believed that one's success mainly came from his hard work not his ability. He also believed that "behavior reform is a central goal of education because virtuous behavior can ensure individual success and societal harmony" (p. 92). Confucius valued pragmatic learning. He viewed the goal of learning as to competently conduct oneself within a civil service job. He stressed the acquisition of essential knowledge and respectful learning. He taught his students to respect and obey authorities. He once said that "to honor those higher than ourselves is the highest expression of the sense of justice" (Confucius, 1947, p. 332).

That is the reason why in Chinese culture, the teachers are always regarded as a model of knowledge and virtue for the students (He, 1996). The teachers do not only teach the students knowledge but also help students choose their future careers. As a Chinese saying goes "One day's teacher, a lifetime master," which means students should always respect the teacher no matter how long he teaches them. Teachers can be very influential in Chinese students' lives.

CESL STUDENTS' PRIOR EDUCATION IN CHINA

Current CESL students studying at North American universities received their elementary, secondary and undergraduate education in China. Chinese education is an examination-driven system. Elementary, secondary, and higher education can be characterized as being very competitive. This competitiveness, according to Huang (1997), has both advantages and disadvantages. On the one hand, it can help produce highly knowledgeable, skilful, and talented individuals. On the other hand, it can create too much stress or pressure and may cause unbalanced development in the students.

Confucian philosophy on education still has a strong impact on the current Chinese educational system. In Confucius' times, one had to pass the imperial examinations in order to become an official. Confucius thought that education was a way for self-development and to ultimately become a useful person to the state. To Chinese people, education is the only way to become successful in society. In China today, people still believe that only college graduates can possess a high status in society. A good education can bring honor to the family and even the community. Parents feel honored if their children can go to colleges and universities. As a result, examinations have become the only way of selecting candidates to study at colleges and universities.

CULTURAL DIFFERENCES AFFECTING CESL STUDENTS' ACADEMIC LEARNING

Bearing the Chinese traditional ideas in mind, the CESL students surely meet certain challenges in their academic studies at North American universities where the cultural environment and educational system are totally different.

Sharing No Common Interest Discouraging Participation

Sharing no common topics and interest is a cultural challenge for CESL students at North American universities. North Americans often talk about football and baseball, for example. But CESL students have no idea about popular North American sports. Due to cultural differences, CESL students often avoid participating in social activities in North America. They feel it is hard to make real North American friends. There is a lack of mutual understanding between CESL students and their North American peers (Feng, 1991).

Chinese Cultural Beliefs Affecting Communication

Liu (1994) indicated that CESL students studying at an American university transfer their Chinese cultural values and beliefs into the American context when communicating with native Americans. In the middle of Huang's (2002) presentation at a conference, a North American professor raised such a question: "Why do my Chinese students always answer 'yes' (in fact sometimes they have not totally understood) when I ask them whether they have understood my assignments or not?" That was because in Chinese culture, it's shameful for a student to say in front of the class that he/she has not understood the teachers' instructions and assignments. The student would rather ask his/her classmates after class than ask the teacher for repetition and re-explanation in class.

North American Religion Producing Confusion

Religion is a big problem for Chinese students at North American universities. In China people are educated not to believe in God. What people in China believe is communism. However, religion is an important part of North American culture. CESL students feel very concerned about how to deal with religion in North America:

This city is very religious. But in China, few people are interested in religion. We grew up in a communist society. We have been educated by communist doctrine since we were little. Of course many people here are friendly, and willing to help foreign students. But, they often talk about God, and try to convince you to believe in God, which make many of us uncomfortable.

Although host families can help you understand American culture. I think they are often too religious. They are so much interested in religion. They give you Bible, and want you to spend time reading the Bible. On Sundays, they take you to local church. I don't like that (Feng, 1991, p. 10).

North America Holidays Increasing Homesickness

Like religion, holidays are also an important part of North American culture. North Americans and Chinese people have very different holidays to celebrate each year. In North America, Christmas, Thanksgiving, Easter, and Halloween are very important holidays. North American people have different traditions for different holidays and their ways to celebrate different holidays are also different. But in China, people celebrate the Spring Festival, the Dragon Boat Festival, the Mid-Autumn Festival, and so on. When the North Americans are celebrating their holidays, CESL students cannot feel that kind of holiday atmosphere and they often isolate themselves from North American culture. When Chinese holidays come, they have to go to school. They are also far from their parents and friends. They cannot feel the right kind of Chinese holiday atmosphere either. In that sense, CESL students at North American universities cannot really enjoy any kind of holidays, which increases their homesickness (Feng, 1991).

North American Students' Behavior Affecting Learning

CESL students often feel uncomfortable with the students' behavior in North American classrooms. Upton (1989) indicates that CESL students at American universities have a negative reaction toward American students' behavior. Students can be late for class. They often ask teachers questions or make jokes in class. All these behaviors are considered rude and disrespectful in Chinese classrooms. In North American classrooms students can challenge the teacher at any time by interrupting the teachers and asking them questions. That makes CESL students feel that students do not show any respect for their teachers. This cultural difference may help people understand why CESL students do not often ask teachers questions in class. That they do not often ask questions does not necessarily mean that they are not actively thinking or learning.

CESL students do not feel comfortable with American students' self-centeredness (Chen, 1985). They do not care much what other people think of them. However, in China, students do care what the teacher and other students think of them. If students cannot correctly answer the teachers' questions in class, they think that they have "lost their face" and feel very embarrassed and even ashamed. They are often afraid of making mistakes. This cultural difference can help people to understand why CESL students are not very active in answering teachers' questions or participating in classroom discussions. Just because they are not active in class does not mean that they do not know anything about the topic being discussed or they cannot come up with good ideas. What they need is self-confidence and encouragement from both the teacher and their North American peers.

Cultural Differences Creating Stresses and Anxiety

Anxiety created by Chinese-North American cultural differences negatively affects CESL students' academic learning (Sun and Chen, 1997). Due to cultural differences they feel it difficult to deal with North American students and professors inside and outside of classrooms. Their unfamiliarity with American university environments often creates stress for them. For example, their lack of experience using such university facilities as computers and libraries cause them anxiety that strongly affect their academic learning.

One major limitation of Sun and Chen's (1997) study is that the 12 subjects participating in the study are not typical or traditional full-time students, but exchange scholars. What Chinese exchange scholars experienced might not be applied to typical or average CESL students who are studying full time at North American universities.

North American Instructional Factors Affecting Lecture Understanding

North America and China have different cultures and traditions. The roles of the teacher, for example, are defined and interpreted differently. Fu (1991) argues that in Chinese culture there is a lack of the spirit of equality in the classrooms. Teachers are regarded not only as authorities in their field of study but also as students' moral mentors. In North American classrooms however, there is an equal relationship between teachers and students. Chinese teachers are always very serious and focus on lecturing, while North American teachers often use humor and varied, informal teaching methods in classroom. Differences in teaching styles have become the biggest cultural difference for CESL students (Upton, 1989).

North American teachers' different teaching styles or methods cause considerable challenges for CESL students in their academic learning. The following instructional factors are identified according to several studies on this topic (Chen, 1985; Huang, 2005; Upton, 1989).

Too Much Student Participation

Teachers spend too much time on classroom discussions or student participation, according to a study by Huang (2005), and, this negatively affects CESL students' understanding of academic lectures. In that particular study, over 80% of the CESL students studying at an American university reported that too much student participation and discussion negatively affected their understanding of academic lectures. Students in general arts programs reported there was more student participation in their classrooms than in science classrooms. Student participation caused more problems for students in arts programs than it did for students of science re understanding academic lectures.

Too Much Group Work

In Chinese classrooms, students tend to work individually due to various reasons: class size (too many students in one classroom); the traditional role of a student (uncomfortable feeling of participating); psychological impact (being afraid of making mistakes and losing face); etc. The Chinese teachers are always explainers, and the Chinese students are just listeners and note takers. There is little group work and classroom discussion there. Many CESL students find difficulties in attending classes at North American schools, where group work and discussions are highly encouraged. Students of arts reported more group work and discussions in their classrooms than students of science. Students of arts agreed that group work caused them more challenges in lecture comprehension than students of science (Huang, 2005).

North American teachers usually regard themselves as students' facilitators of learning but not their authorities of knowledge. They can admit their ignorance on a topic. Generally, they do not easily become angered by students' challenging questions as Chinese teachers would. They give students' freedom in expressing their different ideas. They do not directly give the answer to a particular question. What they stress is students' thinking and discussion. So they encourage students to be active in classroom discussions and praise critical and daring ideas (Upton, 1989).

Failure to Follow the Textbook

American teachers' failure to follow textbooks creates challenges for CESL students. According to Huang (2005), as much as 79.6% of the CESL students reported that their American teachers did not closely follow the textbook while lecturing; and most of them were students in general arts programs. Only 20.4% of them reported that their American teachers closely followed the textbooks while lecturing, and most of these students were students of science. More than 90% of the subjects thought they had more problems in understanding an academic lecture if the teachers failed to follow the textbook, and, on the other hand, they had fewer problems in understanding an academic lecture if they closely followed the textbook. In Chinese culture, textbooks have authority over teachers (Fu, 1991). Teachers always closely follow the textbook while lecturing. The teachers go into details about each chapter of the textbook through each term. While in North America, teachers do not feel constrained to follow the textbook and the syllabus, and they do not "worry about getting sidetracked onto some tangential topic in the middle of a lecture" (Upton, 1989, p. 25) either.

Lecture Organization

The structuring or organizing of a lecture is an essential aspect of its comprehensibility (Chaudron and Richards, 1986). Diamond, Sharp and Ory (1983) suggest that effective lecture preparation and delivery can be arranged under the following three stages: 1) the beginning; 2) the body; and 3) the closing. In the beginning stage, the lecturer usually relates lecture content to previous class material, mentions the background of the current lecture, or gives students a brief introduction of the content of the current lecture. In the body of the lecture, there is some flexibility for the lecturer to present the content. The lecturer can either decide the main points and explain them clearly to the listeners or organize the material in some logical order such as "cause-effect," "time-sequential," etc. During the lecture the lecturer may ask some questions to check on students' understanding of the lecture or ask them to make their comments. In the last stage of the lecture, the lecturer may briefly summarize the content of the lecture or reemphasize what he expects the students to learn from the lecture. In Huang's (2005) study, 79.4% of the CESL students at an American university commented that their American teachers' poor lecture organization negatively influenced their academic lecture comprehension.

Lecture Summary

Chinese teachers usually summarize the main idea of a lecture at the end of it. Lecture summary can reemphasize the important points of a lecture. It can also help students better understand the lecture (Ma and Huang, 1992).

About 55.4% of the CESL students at an American university reported that their teachers never summarized a lecture at the end of it. It was very surprising that 80% of the participants agreed that they could not easily understand the main idea of each lecture if their teachers failed to summarize the lecture at the end of it, because almost every teacher in Chinese universities does so, and, the CESL students had the same expectations for lectures in their North American classrooms (Huang, 2005).

Blackboard Writing

In Chinese classrooms, teachers write a lot on the blackboard while lecturing. They always put the important and difficult points on the blackboard. Blackboard writing can give students a deep impression and help them better understand a lecture (Ma and Huang, 1992). But in North American classrooms, teachers, teachers of arts in particular, do not write much on the board while lecturing. The lack of blackboard writing caused problems for CESL students in understanding academic lectures (Huang, 2005). CESL students are used to point-by-point lectures with outlines and key points put on the blackboard. Upton (1989) mentioned that American university lectures are broad and extensive compared with the "intensive, narrow, and detailed" (p.25) lectures in Chinese classrooms. CESL students often get confused about what they should learn from a lecture.

CESL students expect their North American teachers to give detailed explanations of every topic and put the key points, or outline, on the blackboard in order for them to take detailed notes. When their expectations are not met, they tend to think that their North American teachers are not as resourceful and responsible as their teachers back in China. Actually it is a cultural difference. North American teachers expect their students to do extensive reading and look for related information on their own outside of class (Upton, 1989). However, they may not convey this expectation clearly to their CESL students.

Most instructional factors are based on Huang's (2005) study. The results of this study were based on students' self-report data, which might not represent the real situations. What is more, this study was conducted at only one American university, and, there were only 78 participants in the study. These two factors might affect the generalizibility of the results and limit the researcher's interpretation.

IMPLICATIONS FOR EDUCATION

North American teachers should try to create a better learning environment for culturally different students, and, be aware of the challenges faced by CESL students in the classroom. The use of examples or situations that happen only in North American culture should not be used excessively in the classroom. At the same time, we need to help CESL students understand North American culture and encourage them to actively participate in classroom discussions. Further, we North American teachers may need to adjust our teaching methods in order to make our lectures more accessible to CESL students and other ESL students. For example, we might give students a study guide and write the major points on the blackboard while lecturing. We could also provide students with related materials in advance if we are teaching something not related to the textbook. Sometimes we need to slow down the pace of our lectures and break up content into accessible units. These tactics could be of benefit to North American students as well[1].

REFERENCES

Althen, G. (1999). *Orientation of foreign students.* Working paper #13. Washington, DC: National Association of Foreign Student Affairs. (ERIC Document Reproduction Service No. ED 330 297)

Arthur, N. (1997). Counseling issues with international students. *Canadian Journal of Counseling, 31,* 259-274.

Asada, K., Kiso, K., Yoshikawa, K (1974) Univalent reduction of molecular oxygen by spinach chloroplast on illumination. *Journal of Biological Chemistry.* 249, 2175-2181.

Asada, K (2000) The water-water cycle as alternative photon and electron sinks, *Phill. Trans. stress and R. Soc. Land. B.* 355, 1419-1431.

Bennett, S. (1999). *Comprehensive multicultural education: Theory and practice.* Allyn and Bacon, Boston, MA

Berman, R. and Cheng, L. (2001). English academic language skills: Perceived difficulties by undergraduate and graduate students, and their academic achievement. *Canadian Journal of Applied Linguistics, 4(1-2)*, 25-40.

Bontrager, T., Birch, W. G., and Kracht, J. B. (1990). International students' concerns: Directions of supportive programming. *College Student Affairs Journal, 10(2),* 22-28.

Canadian Bureau for International Education. (2002, April 15). *International student numbers hit record high, but Canada offers dwindling support for African students.* Retrieved October 28, 2002 from the World Wide Web: *http://www.cbie.ca/news/ index_e.cfm?folder=releasesandpage=rel_2002-04-15_e*

Chaudron, C., and Richards, J. C. (1986). The effect of discourse markers on the comprehension of lectures. *Applied Linguistics, 7,* 113-127.

Chen, C. P. (1999). Common stressors among international college students: Research and counseling implications. *Journal of College Conseling, 2,* 49-65.

Chen, T. H. (1985). *Cultural differences in classrooms: A comparison of Chinese and US schooling.* Unpublished manuscript. Confucius. (1947). The wisdom of Confucius. In S.

---

[1] This article was originally published in *Education.*

Commins and R. N. Linscott (Eds.), *Man and man: The social philosophers* (pp. 323-358). New York: Random House.

Clairbone A (1985) Catalase activity. In Greewald, R.A., (Ed.), *Handbook of Methods for Oxygen Radical Research.* (pp. 283-284). CRC press, Boca Raton, Florida.

Deressa, B., and Beaver, I. (1988). Needs assessment of international students in a College of Home Economics. *Educational Research Quarterly, 12,* 51-56.

Desjardins M, Morse D (1993) The polypeptide component of scintillons, the bioluminescent organelles of the dinoflagellate *Gonyaulax polyedra. Biochem Cell Biol.* 71, 176-182.

Dhindsa, R. H., Plumb-Dhindsa, P., Thorpe, T.A. 1981. Leaf senescence correlated with increased level of membrane permeability, lipid peroxidation and decreased level of SOD and CAT. *Journal of Experimental Botany.* 32, 93–101.

Diamond, N. A., Sharp, G. and Ory, J. C. (1983). *Improving your lecturing.* Office of Instructional and Management Services, University of Illinois at Urbana-Champaign.

Feng, J. H. (1991). *The adaptation of Students from the People's Republic of China to an American Academic Culture.* Reports (ERIC Document Reproduction Service No. ED 329 833).

Ferris D. and Tagg, T. (1996). Academic listening/speaking tasks for ESL students: Problems, suggestions, and implications. *TESOL Quarterly, 30,* 297-317.

Fu, D. L. (1991). A process classroom through the eyes of an outsider. *Language Arts, 68,* 121-123.

Foyer CH (1996) Oxygen processing in photosynthesis. *Biochem. Soc. Trans.* 24, 427–433.

Grata˜o, P.L., Polle, A., Lea, P.J., Azevedo, R.A. 2005. Making the life of heavy metal-stressed plants a little easier. *Functional Plant Biology.* 32, 481–494.

He, H. W. (1996). *Chinese students' approach to learning English: Psycholinguistic and sociolinguistic perspectives.* Unpublished master's thesis, Biola University, La Mirada, CA.

Hoagland DR, Arnon DI (1950) The water-culture method for growing plants without soil. *Calif. Agric. Exp. Station Circ.* 347, 1-32.

Huang, J. (1997). *Chinese students and scholars in American higher education.* Praeger Publishers, Westport, CT.

Huang, J. (2002). *An evaluation of Chinese students' English academic listening challenges.* Paper presented at the Gardner Annual Conference. New York.

Huang, J. (2004). Voices from Chinese students: Professors' use of English affects academic listening. *College Student Journal, 38(2),* 212-223.

Huang, J. (2005). Challenges of academic listening in English: Reports by Chinese students. *College Student Journal, 39(3),* 553-569.

Huang, J. (2006). English abilities for academic listening: How confident are Chinese students? *College Student Journal, 40*(1), 218-226.

Huang, J., and Klinger, D. (2006). Chinese graduate students at North American universities: Learning challenges and coping strategies. *The Canadian and International Education Journal, 35(2),* 48-61.

Institute of International Education. (2002, May 16). *98/99 opendoors on the Web.* [Selections from the book], New York. Retrieved June 15, 2002 from the World Wide Web: *http://www.opendoorsweb.org/Lead%20 Stories/intemational_studs.htm*

Leung, C. M. and Berry, J. W. (2001). *The psychological adaptation of international and migrant students in Canada.* Reports-Research (143). (ERIC Document Reproduction Service No. ED 457 795)

Liu, D. L. (1994). *Deep sociocultural transfer and its effect on second language speakers' communication.* Paper presented at the annual meeting of the Teachers of English to Speakers of Other Languages, Maltimore, MD.

Ma, Y, and Huang, J. (1992). *A practical guide to English teaching methodology.* Changsha: Hunan Normal University Press.

Myles, J., Qian, J., and Cheng, L. (2002) International and new immigrant students' adaptations to the social and cultural life at a Canadian university. In S. Bond and C. Bowry (Eds.) *Connections and Complexities: The Internationalization of Canadian Higher Education,* Occasional Papers in *Higher Education,* Vol, 11, Winnipeg, Center for Research and Development in Higher Education.

Nakano Y, Asada K (1981) Hydrogen peroxide is scavenged by ascorbic specific peroxidase in spinach chloroplast. *Plant Cell Physiology.* 22, 867-880.

Owie, I. (1982). Social alienation among foreign students. *College Student Journal, 16,* 163-165.

Palmer, J. A. (2001). *Fifty major thinkers on education.* New York.

Qian, J. (2002). *Chinese graduate students' experiences in writing literature review.* Unpublished master's thesis, Queen's University, Kingston, Ontario.

Shen, J. P. (2001). Confucius. In Joy A. Palmer (Ed.), *Fifty major thinkers on education (pp. 1-5).* New York.Sun, W., and Chen, G. M. (1997). *Dimensions of difficulties Mainland Chinese students encounter in the United States.* Paper presented at the 6th International Conference in Cross-Cultural Communication, Tempe, AZ. (ERIC Document Reproduction Service No. ED 408 635).

Shri, M., Kumar, S., Chakrabarty, D., Trivedi, P.K., Malick, S., Mishra, P., Shukla, D., Mishra, S., Srivastava, S., Tripathi, R.D., Tuli, R (2009) Effect of arsenic on growth, oxidative stress, and antioxidant system in rice seedling. *Ecotoxicoklogy and environmental safety.* 72, 1102-1110.

Trice, A. G. (2001). *Faculty perceptions of graduate international students: The benefits and challenges.* Paper presented at the 26th Annual Meeting of the Association for the Study of Higher Education, Richmond, VA. (ERIC Document Reproduction Service No. ED 457 816).

Tweed R. G., and Lehman, D. R. (2002). Learning considered within a cultural context. *American Psychologist,* Vol, 57, No. 2, 89-99.

Upton, T. A. (1989). Chinese students, American universities, and cultural confrontation. *MinneTESOL Journal, 7,* 9-28.

Velikova V., Yordanov I., Edreva A. (2000) Oxidative stress and some antioxidant systems in acid rain-treated bean plant. *Plant science.* 151, 59-66.

Zhong, M. (1996). *Chinese students and scholars in the US: An intercultural adaptation process.* Paper presented at the 82nd Annual Meeting of the Speech Communication Association, San Diego, CA. (ERIC Document Reproduction Service No. ED 406 704).

In: East Meets West
Editor: Jinyan Huang

ISBN: 978-1-62618-195-3
© 2013 Nova Science Publishers, Inc.

Chapter 7

THE IMPACT OF ACADEMIC SKILLS ON CHINESE ESL STUDENTS' ACADEMIC LISTENING

Jinyan Huang[1,] and Shuangli Su[2]*
[1]Niagara University, Lewiston, New York, US
[2]Untested Ideas Research Center, Niagara Falls, New York, US

ABSTRACT

Research with ESL students has begun to show that Chinese ESL (CESL) students experience particular challenges in English academic listening. This study focuses on their challenges as reported by CESL students in understanding English lectures. Seventy-eight CESL students at an American university participated in this study. This chapter focuses on the effects of the following academic skills on CESL students' lecture comprehension: a) text previewing, b) note-taking, c) short-term memory, and d) English language skills. This chapter also offers suggestions for CESL students about how to improve their academic skills for English lecture comprehension at American universities.

INTRODUCTION

English academic listening comprehension is often difficult for ESL students (Brown, 1994). It places high demands upon listeners. They should have not only the relevant background knowledge but also related academic skills such as note-taking (Flowerdew, 1995). Their difficulty will be reduced if they have effective academic skills and helpful preparation for the lectures (Ferris and Tagg, 1996).

Taking notes is regarded as a useful skill for students to comprehend academic lecture. But "writing down as much as possible" during a lecture may not result in effective encoding of the lecture for note takers. They should compact large amount of spoken discourse into

---

* Correspondence concerning this chapter should be addressed to Dr. Jinyan Huang at *jhuang@niagara.edu*.

propositional-type information units; transcribed content words, symbols, and a limited number of structure words (Dunkel, 1988).

Mason (1995) discusses the fact that academic listening/speaking tasks are growing more complex and difficult for ESL students and they require more than the traditional note-taking and formal speaking skills. They are expected to actively participate in the listening/speaking activities in modern classrooms. They are not just passive listeners or note-takers. They should have active thinking ability and quick response skills.

Dunkel, Mishra, and Berliner (1985) investigate the effects of such academic skills as note-taking, memory, and language proficiency on lecture learning. One hundred and thirty-six native speakers of English and one hundred and twenty-three ESL students from thirty-four foreign countries who were enrolled at an American university participated in this study. The results show that note-taking without review may not facilitate effective English lecture encoding for either native or nonnative speakers of English. The results of this study also suggest that learners' English language proficiency and short-term memory have a significant effect on lecture learning.

If ESL students possess appropriate academic skills, they can better organize the incoming information as they listen to an academic lecture. As they become more aware of their role in selecting important information, students can follow the professor's organizational design, and make predictions about where the lecture is heading. Therefore appropriate academic learning skills become crucially important for ESL students to achieve success in academic listening at American universities.

However, little research has investigated the effects of academic skills on Chinese ESL (CESL) students' English lecture comprehension. This study examined the effects of a variety of factors on CESL students' English lecture comprehension at an American university.

ABOUT THIS STUDY

Seventy-eight CESL students who enrolled in the 2000 winter semester at an American university participated in this study. Among the 78 CESL students, the number of male students (40) and female students (38), and the number of arts students (36) and science students (42), were distributed almost equally; however, the number of undergraduate students (18) and graduate students (60), and the number of students who had studied at this American school for more than one year (56) and those for less than one year (22), were distributed very unequally. All of the 78 participants had achieved a TOEFL (Test of English as a Foreign Language) score greater than 550 before they came to America, and 48 scored greater than 600.

A questionnaire was used as the instrument of the study. It consisted of thirty items and an open-ended question. Among the thirty items, twenty-five required the participants to mark their responses on a five-point Likert scale, three were ranking items, and two were multiple-choice items. The data obtained for the five-point scale items were first analyzed by using descriptive statistical methods. A Factorial ANOVA was then used to determine whether there was a significant difference in the responses according to the following 4 independent variables: a) gender (male/female), b) major (arts/science), c) level of study (undergraduate/ graduate), and d) length of time studying in America (less than one year/more than one year).

If there were significant differences between the independent variables, a descriptive *post hoc* analysis was conducted to see where the differences occurred.

For the ranking items, the percentage of respondents choosing each point on the scale was calculated. Then the standard deviation and mean score of each item were calculated by assigning seven points to the top ranked item, six points to the second place, five points to the third place, etc., in the case of the seven-point items.

For the open-ended question, every response was categorized into groups of similar responses, and categories placed in a frequency order with most frequent at the top. In order to increase the inter-rater reliability, two colleagues of the researcher were invited to categorize all the participants' responses to the open-ended question. Most of the subjects answered the open-ended question in Chinese. The three raters first carefully read all the responses and translated the Chinese responses into English. After that they worked individually to put the similar responses together to form a suggestion.

RESULTS AND DISCUSSION

The effects of other factors on Chinese students' English lecture comprehension have been addressed in Chapters Nine and Ten. This chapter focuses on the effects of such academic skills as text previewing, note-taking, short-term memory, and English language proficiency on their lecture comprehension as reported by CESL students at an American university. The results are summarized in Table 7.1.

Table 7.1. Effects of Academic Skills on CESL Students' Lecture Comprehension

Academic Skills	Number of Responses	Mean	Standard Deviation	Significant Differences $(p < .05)$
Text previewing	78	4.69	0.57	N/A
Note-taking	78	4.14	1.18	③
Short-term memory	78	4.33	0.83	③
Pronunciation	71	2.08	1.64	N/A
Grammar	71	2.55	1.43	N/A
Vocabulary	71	5.51	1.38	N/A
Listening	71	6.48	1.12	N/A
Speaking	71	3.94	1.34	N/A
Reading	71	4.01	1.40	N/A
Writing	71	3.42	1.34	N/A

Note: ① Gender   ② Major   ③ Level of study   ④ Length of time studying in America

The Effects of Text Previewing on Lecture Comprehension

Previewing the text before class is considered by Chinese educators as an effective academic skill for lecture comprehension (Ma and Huang, 1992). The following question was intended to determine the effects of previewing texts on students' lecture comprehension. It read as follows: "Does reading the text before a lecture help you understand a lecture? (1 = not at all, 5 = very much)"

All the 78 participants chose scale points 4 and 5 and, therefore, they agreed that reading the text before a lecture could help them understand the lecture. There was no significant difference between these groups of participants in terms of their gender, major, level of study, and length of time studying in America. Previewing the text can help students become familiar with the background and content of a new lecture, therefore it is considered effective for lecture comprehension (Ma and Huang, 1992).

The Effects of Taking Notes on Lecture Comprehension

The question was to investigate the effects of the academic skill of taking notes on CESL students' understanding of English lectures. It read as follows: "Does the skill of taking notes in class help you understand a lecture? (1 = not at all, 5 = very much)"

For this question, on the one hand, as many as 80.8% of participants (who chose scale points 4 and 5) agreed that the academic skill of taking notes in class helped them understand a class lecture. Taking notes while listening to the teacher, according to Ma and Huang (1992), can concentrate students' mind and help them distinguish more important points from less important ones. Students can also use notes to review the lecture after class. On the other hand, only 6.4% of the participants (who chose scale point 2) did not think taking notes in class was an effective academic skill for lecture comprehension.

Statistical analysis indicates significant differences in participants' responses to this question between undergraduate students and graduate students ($p < .05$). Undergraduate students (mean = 4.94) agreed more strongly than graduate students (mean = 3.90) that the academic skill of taking notes in class helped them comprehend a class lecture. There was no difference between the other three independent variables.

The Effects of Short-term Memory on Lecture Comprehension

Related literature shows that good short-term memory helps students understand a lecture (Dunkel, Mishra, and Berliner, 1985). In order to investigate the effects of short-term memory on CESL students' English lecture comprehension, the following question was asked: "Does good short-term memory help you understand a lecture? (1 = not at all, 5 = very much)"

The results show that 83.3% of the participants (who chose scale points 4 and 5) thought good short term memory could help them understand a class lecture. It was very surprising that no participants chose scale points 1 and 2, indicating that there was no objection to the statement.

Statistical analysis shows significant differences in participants' responses to this question between undergraduate students and graduate students ($p < .05$). Undergraduate students (mean = 4.83) agreed more strongly than graduate students (mean = 4.18) that good short term memory helped them understand a lecture. There was no significant difference between the other three independent variables.

The Effects of Language Components on Lecture Comprehension

It is known to all that ESL students' English language abilities directly affect their comprehension of an English lecture. This question was intended to investigate the effects of English language components on CESL students' comprehension of English lectures. It read as follows: "In general, what components of your English language abilities do you think affect your comprehension of a lecture? Please rank the following as 7 = highest, 1 = lowest. pronunciation [ ] grammar [ ] vocabulary [ ] listening [ ] speaking [ ] reading [ ] writing [ ]"

The results are summarized in Table 7.2.

Fewer than 78 participants responded to this item. This is because some of them misunderstood the instructions and gave the same ranking to two or more components. The participants were originally asked to give each component a different ranking.

Table 7.2 shows that there was a clear hierarchy among the components of the participants' English language abilities affecting their comprehension of an English lecture. The rank order was 1) listening, 2) vocabulary, 3) speaking, 4) reading, 5) writing, 6) grammar, and 7) pronunciation.

On the one hand, CESL students ranked that their listening skills (mean = 6.48) and amount of vocabulary (mean = 5.51) had the most effects on their understanding of an English academic lecture. Quite a few participants commented at the end of this item that their small vocabulary really negatively affected their lecture comprehension. On the other hand, pronunciation (mean = 2.08) and grammar knowledge (mean = 2.55) were ranked to have the least effects on their comprehension of an English lecture by the CESL students.

Table 7.2. Respondents' Rankings of Effects of Language Components on Lecture Comprehension

	Responses and percent selecting each							Summary statistics		
	1	2	3	4	5	6	7	N	Mean	Sd
Pronunciation	53.5	24.0	7.1	2.8	4.2	5.6	2.8	71	2.08	1.64
Grammar	18.3	52.1	5.6	9.9	11.3	0	2.8	71	2.55	1.43
Vocabulary	0	8.5	5.6	4.2	1.4	69.0	11.3	71	5.51	1.38
Listening	1.4	0	2.8	2.8	4.2	15.5	73.3	71	6.48	1.12
Speaking	5.6	9.9	22.5	14.1	43.7	2.8	1.4	71	3.94	1.34
Reading	7.1	1.4	24.0	36.6	21.1	1.4	8.4	71	4.01	1.40
Writing	14.1	4.2	32.4	29.6	14.1	5.6	0	71	3.42	1.34

Note: The most frequently selected response in each category is in bold face.

PRACTICLA SUGGESTIONS FOR CESL STUDENTS

In order to elicit CESL students' frank opinions and practical suggestions concerning how to improve their academic skills for English lecture comprehension, an open-ended question was asked at the end of the questionnaire. The open-ended question asked the participants to give suggestions for both CESL students and their American professors.

Table 7.3 is a summary of the suggestions for CESL students. The numbers after each suggestion indicates the number of participants who gave the suggestion. Suggestions were listed together if there was a tie.

In total, 16 suggestions were raised for CESL students. Arts students offered more suggestions than science students. Twenty-five participants (32%) suggested that CESL students get well acquainted with American culture by every possible means. For example, they should create every possible opportunity to talk to native speakers of English in order to understand their language and culture. Other suggestions for CESL students required them to use appropriate learning skills or strategies and get themselves actively involved in the classroom learning processes.

Table 7.3. Suggestions for CESL Students

1. Improve listening ability by making American friends, watching TV, etc. (7)
2. Make more efforts to get well acquainted with the American culture. (7)
3. Expose to more English speaking environment. (6)
4. Practice English with native speakers. (5)
5. Be well prepared for any class lecture. (4)
6. Go over what has been learned in a timely manner. (4)
7. Frequently communicate with American teachers. (4)
8. Always preview the texts and try to get familiar with the background materials. (4)
9. Have confidence in academic listening. (3)
10. Get used to American classroom teaching style. (3)
11. Actively participate in classroom discussions. (3)
12. Don't hesitate to ask the teacher questions about a lecture. (3)
13. Try to sit near the front of the class in order to see the board and hear the teacher. (2)
14. Feel free to ask either the teacher or peers for clarification about a lecture. (2)
15. Edit and review class notes as soon as possible after class. (2)
16. Focus on the main idea of a lecture instead of some minor details. (1)

CONCLUSION

This paper[1] investigated the effects of such academic skills as text previewing, note-taking, short-term memory, and English language proficiency on their lecture comprehension as reported by CESL students at an American university. First, all the 78 participants agreed that previewing the text before class was an effective academic skill for lecture comprehension.

Second, more than 80% of participants thought that taking notes in class and good short-term memory helped them understand a class lecture. Finally, listening skills and amount of vocabulary were ranked to have the most effects on their understanding of an English academic lecture by the participants.

Although this study was conducted only with the CESL students at one American university, the results may be applied to the CESL students in other American schools and the Chinese students who are still in China and want to study at American universities. This is because all the Chinese students who are studying or will study at American schools have similar educational and cultural backgrounds. They may experience similar challenges in understanding English academic lectures. In order to better prepare for academic listening, they should be aware of some effective academic skills or strategies which can help them

---

[1] This article was originally published in *College Student Journal.*

become successful academic listeners. For example, they should preview before each lecture and review after it. Taking notes is also an effective classroom learning strategy. They can write down the important points of each lecture. These notes can help them review and reinforce the previous lectures. Additionally, they need to expose themselves to more English lecture environment, and learn appropriate skills and strategies for understanding both the content and the organization of the material presented in the lectures.

REFERENCES

Brown, H. D. (1994). *Teaching by principles.* New Jersey: Prentice Hall Agents.

Dunkel, P. (1988). The content of L1 and L2 students' lecture notes and its relation to test performance. *TESOL Quarterly, 22,* 259-279.

Dunkel, P., Mishra, S., and Berliner, D. (1985). Effects of note-taking, memory, and language proficiency on lecture learning for native and nonnative speakers of English. *TESOL Quarterly, 23,* 543-549.

Ferris D., and Tagg, T. (1996). Academic listening/speaking tasks for ESL students: Problems, suggestions, and implications. *TESOL Quarterly, 30,* 297-317.

Flowerdew, J. (1995). Research of relevance to second language lecture comprehension: An overview. In J. Flowerdew (Ed.), *Academic listening: Research perspectives* (pp. 7-29). Cambridge: Cambridge University Press.

Huang, J. (2004). Voices from Chinese students: Professors' use of English affects academic listening. *College Student Journal, 38*(2), 212-223.

Huang, J. (2005). Challenges of academic listening in English: Reports by Chinese students. *College Student Journal, 39*(3), 553-569.

Ma, Y. C., and Huang, J. (1992). *A practical guide to English teaching methodology.* Changsha: Hunan Normal University Press.

Mason, A. (1995). By dint of: Student and lecturer perceptions of lecture comprehension strategies in first-term graduate study. In J. Flowerdew (Ed.), *Academic listening: Research perspectives* (pp. 199-218). Cambridge: Cambridge University Press.

In: East Meets West
Editor: Jinyan Huang

ISBN: 978-1-62618-195-3
© 2013 Nova Science Publishers, Inc.

Chapter 8

THE MERGING OF TWO CULTURES IN THE CLASSROOM

Jinyan Huang[1] and Shuangli Su[2]*
[1]Niagara University, Lewiston, New York, US
[2]Untested Ideas Research Center, Niagara Falls, New York, US

ABSTRACT

This chapter reports a study that investigated four Chinese ESL (CESL) graduate students' perceptions of the major differences between North American and Chinese classroom teaching styles. Major differences in the following five areas were identified: a) the teacher's role, b) the student's role, c) the form of class organization, d) the teacher's expectations, and e) the student's expectations. It then explored these four CESL graduate students' North American classroom learning reality. Finally, the study examined how they adjusted their classroom learning strategies and approaches accordingly so that they could adapt to the North American classroom environment.

INTRODUCTION

During the past two decades there has been a significant growth in the number of non-native speakers (NNS) of English pursuing academic studies in North American universities. Statistics shows that students from the People's Republic of China are the largest single group, and approximately 80% of them are graduate students (Canadian Bureau for International Education, 2002; Institute of International Education, 2001). Generally, they have completed their undergraduate education in China prior to commencing graduate studies in North American universities. Chinese ESL (CESL) graduate students are from a very different cultural background. Their learning experience in North American classrooms has important educational implications for both university administrators and educators.

---

* Correspondence concerning this chapter should be addressed to Dr. Jinyan Huang at *jhuang@niagara.edu*.

Academic learning, as argued by Tweed and Lehman (2002), varies depending on the cultural context. They proposed a Confucian-Socratic framework to analyze the influence of different cultural contexts on academic learning. Socrates (469-399 BC), a Western exemplar, valued the questioning of both his own and others' beliefs, the evaluation of others' knowledge, self-generated knowledge, and teaching by implanting doubt. Socratic-oriented learning involves "overt and private questioning, expression of personal hypotheses, and a desire for self-directed tasks" (p. 93). In contrast, Confucius (551-479 BC), an Eastern exemplar, valued effortful and respectful learning, behavioral reform, and pragmatic acquisition of essential knowledge (Tweed and Lehman, 2002). Confucian-oriented learning involves "effort-focused conceptions of learning, pragmatic orientations to learning, and acceptance of behavioral reform as an academic goal" (p. 93).

Confucian philosophy has a strong impact on Chinese people's viewpoints, ways of thinking and behaviors. Confucius stressed the importance of hard work. He believed that success was mainly due to hard work rather than ability. He also believed that "behavior reform is a central goal of education because virtuous behavior can ensure individual success and societal harmony" (Tweed and Lehman, 2002, p. 92). Confucius valued pragmatic learning. He viewed the goal of learning as to competently conduct oneself within a civil service job. He stressed the acquisition of essential knowledge and respectful learning. He taught his students to respect and obey authorities. He once said that "to honor those higher than ourselves is the highest expression of the sense of justice" (Confucius, 1947, p.332).

When CESL graduate students come to study in North American classrooms, many bring a Confucian-oriented perspective to their learning, while their North American professors and peers may have a more Socratic orientation. Since they have little exposure to Western classroom cultures, they will feel unfamiliar and even uncomfortable with North American classroom culture.

Research with NNS of English studying at North American universities in an English for academic purposes context has indicated that CESL graduate students experience considerable challenges and anxiety in their academic studies (Huang, 2004, 2005; Huang and Klinger, 2006; Sun and Chen, 1997; Upton, 1989). They often feel uncomfortable with the students' behaviors at North American classrooms (Upton, 1989). Students can be late for class. They often ask teacher questions or make jokes in class. All these behaviors are considered rude and disrespectful in Chinese classrooms. Cultural differences in the classroom create anxiety which negatively affect their achievement (Sun and Chen, 1997). For example, their unfamiliarity with student attitudes, classroom interactions, and teaching methodology increases their anxiety and stress.

Difference in teaching style has become the biggest cultural difference for CESL students (Upton, 1989). The roles of the teacher, for example, are defined and interpreted differently in both cultures. Fu (1991) argues that there is lack of the spirit of equality in Chinese classrooms. Teachers are regarded not only as authorities in their field of study but also the students' moral mentor. Chinese teachers are very serious and focus on lecturing. In contrast, there is generally an equal relationship between teachers and students in North American classrooms. North American teachers often use humor and varied informal teaching methods in classroom (Upton, 1989).

Using a questionnaire, Huang (2005) investigated the impact of classroom instructional factors on 78 CESL students' lecture understanding at an American university. The participants of the study reported that the following instructional factors affected their lecture understanding. First, contrary to their expectations, over 60% of the participants reported that American professors' poor lecture organization influenced their lecture comprehension. Second, more than half of the participants reported that American professors did not closely follow the textbook while lecturing and their failure to follow textbooks created challenges for lecture comprehension. Third, three-fourths of the participants reported that their American teachers did not write much on the board while lecturing, which negatively affected their lecture comprehension. Fourth, more than 65% of the participants reported that their American teachers did not usually provide lecture summaries. However, they believed that lecture summaries facilitated their understanding of lectures. Finally, CESL students reported that there was usually too much student participation and group work in the classrooms. This is perhaps because Socratic-oriented American professors value questioning, discussing, and group work (Tweed and Lehman, 2002). As reported by CESL students, student participation and group work distracted their attention and therefore negatively affected their lecture comprehension (Huang, 2005).

However, the results of this study were based on students' self-report data, which might not represent the real situations. For example, the participants might have not told the truth when they responded to the questionnaire. It is also possible that they might have not become aware of these instructional factors. Further, this study was conducted only at one American university. All these factors might affect the interpretation and generalizibility of the results.

All these studies examined CESL students' cross-cultural learning in general. However, the exact nature of their cross-cultural classroom learning experiences and their levels of satisfaction with and concerns about their classroom learning at North American universities have not been closely examined. Hence, the purpose of this study was to mirror the reality of CESL graduate students' classroom learning at North American universities. The Confucian-Socratic framework (Tweed and Lehman, 2002) was used to analyze the influence of different cultural contexts on their classroom learning at North American universities as reported by CESL graduate students.

ABOUT THIS STUDY

The following three questions informed the study: a) what are CESL graduate students' perceptions of the major differences between North American and Chinese classroom teaching styles? b) what is the reality of their North American classroom learning? and c) how do they adjust their classroom learning strategies and approaches accordingly? Because the purpose of this study was to obtain in-depth information about CESL graduate students' classroom learning reality, semi-structured interviews were conducted. A random purposive sampling strategy was used to select participants because it added credibility to the study (Gay and Airasian, 2003). A sample of four CESL graduate students, two from an American university (participants *A* and *B*) and two from a Canadian university (participants *C* and *D*) participated in the study.

At the time of the interview participant *A* was a Masters of Arts (MA) student majoring in Teaching English to Speakers of Other Languages (TESOL). He came to the American university to study for his MA in August 1998. He was in his fifth year of study and was preparing to graduate shortly.

Participant *B* was a Ph.D. student majoring in Educational Leadership. He came to the same American university in August 1998, and started his Master's program in September. He received his MA in 2000 and then continued to work towards his Ph.D. degree in the same area. He was in the final year of his doctoral program.

Participant *C* was a Master's student majoring in Education. She had started her graduate program at a Canadian university approximately two months before the interview.

Lastly, participant *D* was a Ph.D. student majoring in Mechanical Engineering. He started his Ph.D. program at the same Canadian university in May 2002.

The interviews were conducted face-to-face with the students at the Canadian university and via telephone with those at the American university. These interviews allowed the students to describe the "reality" of their classroom learning experiences at these two North American universities, identifying their perceptions of the main differences between North American and Chinese classroom teaching methodologies and the way they adjust their classroom learning strategies and approaches. In order to investigate the participants' perceptions of the main differences between North American and Chinese classroom teaching methodologies, responses were sorted, categorized, and analyzed under the following five themes: 1) the teacher's role, 2) the student's role, 3) the form of class organization, 4) the teacher's expectations, and 5) the student's expectations.

RESULTS AND DISCUSSION

The results of the interviews are summarized below. As described above, five major differences between North American and Chinese classroom teaching styles were identified: a) the teacher's role, b) the student's role, c) the form of class organization, d) the teacher's expectations, and e) the student's expectations. Further, their North American classroom learning reality was explored. Lastly, the way they adjusted their classroom learning strategies and approaches was examined.

Major Differences between North American and Chinese Classroom Teaching Styles

The Teacher's Role

All participants agreed that the teachers are regarded not only as authorities in their field of study but also students' moral mentor in Confucian-oriented Chinese culture, whereas the Socratic-oriented North American teachers usually regard themselves as facilitators of learning rather than authorities of knowledge. They stress student thinking and discussion, encouraging students to be active in classroom discussions and praising critical and daring ideas (Upton, 1989). As was stated by participant *A*, "Here, the teacher is a stimulator, a supporter. In China, the teacher is a lecturer, a giver."

The Student's Role

All participants agreed that the student's job in the Confucian-oriented Chinese classroom is to listen to the teacher, take notes when necessary, and learn by heart what the teacher has taught, whereas in the Socratic-oriented classroom, the student's job is to actively participate in the classroom discussions, ask questions at any time, and even challenge the teacher.

Chinese classrooms lack the spirit of equality (Fu, 1991). Chinese teachers do not usually stress the importance of students' feedback. But in North American classrooms, teachers value students' feedback. Participant *D* made the following comments:

"The Canadian professors pay attention to the student-teacher interaction in class. Student's feedback is also important for the professor. In Chinese classroom there is a lack of equal relationship between the student and the professor. The Chinese professors have powers over their students. Here things are different. Students can ask their professor questions at any time and they can also challenge their professor's ideas or even correct their professor's mistakes. In Chinese classrooms students are not supposed to challenge their teachers."

The Form of Class Organization

Chinese teachers are very serious and tend to lecture as a teaching style. In contrast, North American teachers often use humor and varied informal teaching methods and they encourage a vast amount of student participation and discussion (Upton, 1989). All the four participants stated that Chinese teachers tend to organize a class in a more formal way or in a step-by-step format, whereas, North American teachers prefer a more informal and casual manner in organizing a class. As noted by participant *A*, "the [North American] teacher doesn't play a critical role in the classroom. The students are playing the most important role in the classroom." Participant *B* further commented that:

"In China, teachers take the full responsibility in the classrooms, they use the cramming method. The teachers mainly lecture in class. Students are very passive. They just listen to the teacher. The teachers do not encourage students' participation. Here things are quite different. Teachers encourage students to think. Students' participation is highly encouraged here. They are motivated to join in the class discussions."

The Teacher's Expectations

In different cultures, the teachers have different expectations. The participants stated that the teachers expect their students to be attentive listeners in Chinese classrooms. But in North American classrooms, the teachers have very different expectations. As was stated by participant *A*, "students are expected to have read all the required materials before they come to the classrooms. The teacher can ask questions according to the materials, and sometimes explain some difficult and important points. The teacher is only an assistant." Participant *B* continued to comment that:

"The [North American] professors encourage student participation and independent thinking in the classroom. Sometimes they like to be challenged by their students. They expect that their students can think critically because critical thinking helps students become creative."

The Student's Expectations

Similarly, as stated by all participants, students have different expectations in Confucian- and Socratic-oriented classrooms. In Confucian-oriented classrooms, for example, students expect teacher's detailed explanation of the text, pointing out the important points, and summarizing the key points of the lecture. However, in Socratic-oriented classrooms, students expect their teachers to give them opportunities to ask questions, express their ideas, and to discuss and debate these ideas. Participant *C* commented that:

"The major difference is student participation in class. In Chinese classrooms, there is very little student participation (I guess, about 10%). But in Canadian classrooms, there is a vast amount of student participation (I guess, at least it's 50%). Most students here are very active and cooperative."

Their North American Classroom Learning Reality

Due to the fact that humanities or social science is more society specific and engineering or science is more universal, CESL graduate students of humanities or social science have more challenges in adapting to the North American classroom learning environment than CESL graduate students of engineering or science because what the former have learned in China does not help them to learn what is learned in North America (Huang, 2005; Huang and Klinger, 2006). Participants *A*, *B*, and *C*, who were social science graduate students in the study, stated that their North American classroom learning experiences were very challenging. They made the following comments:

"It is totally different from China. In the classroom here, the teacher doesn't teach much. Most of the class time is spent on self-reading and group discussion. The teacher doesn't play a critical role in the classroom. The students are playing the most important role in the classroom. Everyone has got to talk and give presentations. But the topics discussed in the classroom are very context-embedded. We are from Chinese culture and have limited knowledge about American culture. Therefore, my classroom learning was very challenging, especially in the first year." (Participant *A*)

"When I first came here, I was not used to the classroom teaching. Teachers [here] encourage students to think. Students' participation is highly encouraged in American classrooms. Students are motivated to join in the class discussions. So we Chinese students feel difficult to be part of the classroom discussions. As a result we feel very disappointed and frustrated." (Participant *B*).

"The classroom learning [here] is very different from the classroom learning in China. The professors here do not talk as much as Chinese professors do. Students here ask more questions. I have anxiety in classroom learning situation here, especially in the first few weeks." (Participant *C*)

However, Participant *D*, who was a Mechanical Engineering graduate student, stated that he had a very pleasant and positive classroom learning experience in general. He did not encounter much difficulty in understanding the lectures. But he found that his English speaking skill was not good enough for him to make oral presentations in the classroom. He made the following comments:

"In Canada, classroom atmosphere is more harmonious. Students communicate just like friends. There is also more students' participation or discussions. Canadian professors expect that students make active response to what they are teaching in class. Students can ask questions at any time. Professors are usually happy to answer students' questions and also ask students further questions to check students' understanding. I did not find any difficulty in following professors' lectures, because I am quite familiar with the content area. ... The biggest obstacle for my classroom learning is related to [my] spoken English. I am not very confident in using English to make oral presentations, which is a common requirement for graduate students [here]."

Adjusting Their Classroom Learning Strategies and Approaches

In response to their classroom challenges and frustrations, all participants stated that it was very important for them to adjust their classroom learning strategies and approaches accordingly so that they could adapt to the North American classroom environment. Participant *A* was fortunate to meet with a North American student who had previous experience with Chinese students. This student involved participant *A* in small group discussions and would continually ask participant *A* to express his questions or ideas. The other participants made the following comments:

"[I need to] get adaptive to American classroom learning context as soon as possible; take full responsibility of learning; become an active learner; spend more time before classes preparing; read extensively about a topic; ask questions whenever possible in class; and actively participate in class discussions. ... Learning strategies I acquired in China are still effective here in America: preview, review, listen to the teacher carefully in class, taking notes, [etc.]. ... I think that memorization is important. Basic things, common knowledge should be memorized. Memorization should be based on comprehension and also should lead to better comprehension." (Participant *B*)

"I am still trying to adjust my learning strategies. For example, I am trying to talk more and participate more in group work. Also when I am reading I try to think of some questions and topics in the reading material. I can then talk and participate in the classroom [discussions]. ... I am also learning to think critically because the professors here often ask us to make critical comments on journal articles. To be very honest, I am not used to critical thinking. It may due to the teaching system in China or my own personality. ... I have started to use some effective reading strategies in the classroom. For reading, for example, I try to look at the key words, the titles, the subtitles, the introduction and the summary, the topic sentence, the first paragraph and the last paragraph so that I can get a rough idea of the materials before I start to read carefully." (Participant *C*)

"[The] self-study ability is very important. In the classroom here, I have to be active all the time. First, I need to be active in thinking and try to understand the lecture. Second, I need to be active in group discussions. Finally, I need to be active in asking and answering questions. Further, note-taking is also an effective strategy for classroom learning. I need to improve my note-taking skills so that I can write down the important points and at the same time I understand the lecture." (Participant *D*)

When asked to provide three suggestions for Chinese students who want to come to North America for graduate studies, the four participants responded that the Chinese students should be psychologically prepared for the academic culture differences: different classroom teaching styles, different student-teacher relationship, and different teacher expectations in North American classrooms. At the same time, adjusting as quickly as possible to the new environment and new classroom teaching style and understanding North American academic culture to minimize cultural shock upon arrival are on the list.

The last interview question asked of the four participants' self-evaluation of their cross-cultural classroom learning experience at these two North American universities. All four found the experience to be very challenging, but positive and beneficial to their graduate study.

CONCLUSION

Guided by the Confucian-Socratic framework (Tweed and Lehman, 2002), this study first investigated four CESL graduate students' perceptions of the major differences between North American and Chinese classroom teaching styles. Major differences in the following five areas were identified: a) the teacher's role, b) the student's role, c) the form of class organization, d) the teacher's expectations, and e) the student's expectations. It then explored the four CESL graduate students' North American classroom learning reality. Their classroom learning, as was stated by the participants, was both challenging and rewarding. It was challenging because the North American classroom learning environment is different. This is best viewed in the difference between the Confucian and Socratic philosophies of learning. Finally, it examined how these four CESL graduate students adjusted their classroom learning strategies and approaches accordingly so that they could adapt to the North American classroom environment. All participants developed effective classroom learning strategies. These strategies focused largely on becoming more active in the classroom and doing more preparatory class work.

The results of the study[2] showed no big differences by both graduate program and the country where the university is located. All participants' overall evaluations of their North American cross-cultural classroom learning experience were both challenging and positive.

The results are important for those CESL students who are currently completing or hope to begin their graduate studies in North American universities. The results also have implications for North American professors who are responsible for these students. It is suggested that this study be replicated at more North American universities where there are CESL graduate students to validate findings of this study. A slight variation might include interviewing some North American professors who have CESL graduate students in their classes or who supervise CESL graduate students.

REFERENCES

Canadian Bureau for International Education. (2002, April 15). *International student numbers hit record high, but Canada offers dwindling support for African students.* Retrieved October 28, 2002 from the World Wide Web:*http://www.cbie.ca/news/index_e.cfm? folder=releasesandpage=rel_2002-04-15_e*

Confucius. (1947). The wisdom of Confucius. In S. Commins and R. N. Linscott (Eds.), *Man and man: The social philosophers (pp. 323-358).* New York: Random House. (Original work published ca. 479 B. C. E.)

---

[2] This article was originally published in *Journal of Instructional Psychology.*

Fu, D. L. (1991). A process classroom through the eyes of an outsider. *Language Arts, 68,* 121-123.

Gay, L. R., and Airasian, P. (2003). *Educational research: Competencies for analysis and applications.* Prentice Hall: New Jersey.

Huang, J. (2004). Voices from Chinese students: Professors' use of English affects academic listening. *College Student Journal, 38*(2), 212-223.

Huang, J. (2005). Challenges of academic listening in English: Reports by Chinese students. *College Student Journal, 39*(3), 553-569.

Huang, J., and Klinger, D. (2006). Chinese graduate students at North American universities: Learning challenges and coping strategies. *The Canadian and International Education Journal, 35*(2), 48-61.

Institute of International Education. (2001, May 16). *98/99 opendoors on the Web.* [Selections from the book], New York. Retrieved June 15, 2002 from the World Wide Web: *http://www.opendoorsweb.org/Lead%20Stories/international_studs.htm*

Sun, W. and Chen, G. M. (1997). *Dimensions of difficulties Mainland Chinese students encounter in the United States.* Paper presented at the 6th International Conference in Cross-Cultural Communication, Tempe, AZ. (ERIC Document Reproduction Service No. ED 408 635)

Tweed R. G., and Lehman, D. R. (2002). Learning considered within a cultural context. *American Psychologist, 57*(2), 89-99.

Upton, T. A. (1989). Chinese students, American universities, and cultural confrontation. *Minne TESOL Journal, 7,* 9-28.

PART 3: WEST MEETS EAST

In: East Meets West
Editor: Jinyan Huang

ISBN: 978-1-62618-195-3
© 2013 Nova Science Publishers, Inc.

Chapter 9

NORTH AMERICAN PROFESSORS' USE OF ENGLISH AFFECTS CHINESE ESL STUDENTS' ACADEMIC LISTENING

Jinyan Huang[1] and Shuangli Su[2]*
[1]Niagara University, Lewiston, New York, US
[2]Untested Ideas Research Center, Niagara Falls, New York, US

ABSTRACT

Research in English for Academic Purposes has begun to show that non-native speakers of English have much difficulty in English academic listening at American universities. Chinese ESL (CESL) students, who are from a very different educational system and cultural environment, experience special challenges in English academic listening. This chapter focuses on how American professors' use of English in class affects CESL students' understanding of academic lectures. Seventy-eight CESL students who enrolled in the 2000 winter semester at an American university participated in this study. The results show that a) the rapidness of professors' English speech; b) professors' lack of clear pronunciation; c) professors' use of long and complex sentences; d) professors' use of colloquial and slang expressions; e) professors' lack of clear definition of terms and concepts; and f) professors' use of discourse markers affect CESL students' English academic listening at an American university. It offers important suggestions for American professors as how to make their lectures more accessible to CESL students.

SPECIAL REQUIREMENTS OF ACADEMIC LISTENING

To further increase the challenges, academic listening is different from everyday conversational listening. Flowerdew (1995) discusses the following distinct characteristics and demands placed upon listeners in academic situations.

---

* Correspondence concerning this chapter should be addressed to Dr. Jinyan Huang at *jhuang@niagara.edu*.

First, academic listening requires some relevant background information. The listeners will have more difficulty in understanding an academic lecture if they lack background knowledge about the topic of the lecture. Sometimes American professors mention many unfamiliar examples or situations that happen only in American culture, making it difficult for ESL students from different cultures to understand the lecture.

Second, because an academic lecture contains both important and unimportant information on the topic discussed, academic listening requires the listeners to be able to distinguish between what is relevant and what is not relevant. Some lectures are carefully planned, and they are usually predictable. But some academic lectures are full of free discussions and frequent questions and answers. In these situations, students must possess the ability to get the important and relevant information and ignore the rest.

Third, academic listening contains a certain amount of implied meaning or indirect speech acts. That is to say, the students are required to be able to understand the real meaning through the context. Sometimes they should also learn to recognize some instructional tasks such as warnings, suggestions, and advice.

Fourth, academic listening contains long stretches of talk, and the listeners don't have the opportunity of engaging in the facilitating functions of interactive discourse, so it places high demands upon listeners. To succeed, they must learn to identify relationships among units within discourse such as main ideas, supporting ideas, and examples.

Flowerdew and Miller (1997) further outline some additional important features that differentiate authentic lecture discourse from written text or scripted lectures. An authentic lecture is often structured according to "tone groups" and in the form of incomplete clauses. It is often signaled by "micro-level discourse markers" such as "and," "so," "but," "now," "okay." What's more, in an authentic lecture, speakers use many false starts, hesitations, corrections and repetition. The speakers do not usually organize their thoughts well and, at the same time, present what they want to say in complete grammatical sentences. This actually makes it difficult for the listeners to process what they need to understand.

Finally, speakers use gestures and facial expressions in delivering a lecture. These body and facial movements, which provide additional clues about the lecture but are culturally based, may be misunderstood by the listeners and appear to be problematic for them. So the students must be able to recognize the functions of non-verbal cues when they are listening to an academic lecture.

Ferris and Tagg (1996) comment that there is frequent "give" and "take" between teacher and students in an academic classroom situation. This includes formal, planned lecture material, informal questions or comments from the students, and unplanned responses to students by the professor. During these give-and-take activities, students become more involved. On the one hand, they have to actively participate in these activities; on the other hand they have to comprehend what is going on in class and try to get the important points of the lecture. So understanding the lecture may place an even greater burden on non-native speakers than the traditional "chalk-and-talk" lecture, which is carefully planned, and usually, predictable.

From the above discussions we can conclude that academic listening tasks, compared with general listening tasks, place much higher demands upon the listeners, and that academic listening tasks pose formidable challenges for L2 students, even those highly proficient in English (Ferris and Tagg, 1996).

EFFECTS OF DISCOURSE MARKERS ON
LECTURE COMPREHENSION

Discourse markers signal the information structure of discourse by emphasizing directions and relations within classroom discourse (Chaudron and Richards, 1985). A number of markers of the rhetorical organization of lecture discourse are identified by Murphy and Candlin (1979), including what they refer to as starters (*well now let's get on with...*), and metastatements (*I want to mention two types of ...*). These discourse markers, which are often used by academic lecturers, are called "macro markers." Some research suggests that the lecturer's use of signals such as *well, so, now,* which serve as pause or hesitation fillers, are called "micro markers". According to a study by Chaudron and Richards (1985), macro markers, the higher order discourse markers signaling major transitions and emphasis in the lectures, are more conducive to successful recall of the lecture than micro markers, which are lower order markers of segmentation and intersentential connections.

Studies have shown that non-native English-speaking learners have difficulties in recognizing these discourse markers within lectures. Yuan (1982) conducted a study on Chinese scientists' difficulties in comprehending English science lectures at UCLA. The subjects in this study were five Chinese scholars who were studying at UCLA. The subjects were asked to watch a new videotape-based English science lecture. They were allowed to take notes. After that they were asked to answer macro and micro questions prepared by the researcher in advance. The results of this study showed that the subjects, generally, "were rather weak at paying attention to the sequence of the lecture because of their neglect of the logical connectors of sequence and their lack of recognition of transition from one main idea to another. Additionally, they paid more attention to decoding the speech sentence by sentence than to extracting the science information from the lecture through understanding the rhetorical nature and functions of both textual and lecture discourse" (p.48).

The use of macromarkers by the lecturer can help students understand a lecture better if the students understand them. Chaudron and Richards (1985) comment that it is important to realize that lectures read from a written text will usually lack the kinds of macromarkers found in the more conversational style of teaching. An academic lecture that uses more macromarkers is likely to be easier for learners to follow, but an overuse of macromarkers possibly distracts from the overall coherence of the lecture.

We can conclude that the use of discourse markers that indicate the overall organization of a lecture can help non-native speakers, including CESL students, comprehend an academic lecture better if they understand the markers. Similarly, their lack of recognition of discourse markers can create more challenges for them in understanding an academic lecture.

CESL STUDENTS' CHALLENGES IN LISTENING
TO ENGLISH LECTURES

Research shows that some difficulties in understanding and remembering information from lectures may be due to the lack of English language skill itself. Brown (1994) points out three linguistic sources which make listening difficult: a) the use of colloquial language; b) the use of reduced forms; and c) the "prosodic features" of the English language.

Colloquial language is a special challenge. Brown points out that ESL learners who have been exposed to standard written English and "textbook" language sometimes find it surprising and difficult to deal with colloquial language, because the speakers often use many colloquial and slang expressions such as "Don't be a slacker;" "Don't let homework get above your head;" "to be on the ball;" "to stay on top of it;" etc. It is a real challenge for ESL learners to be reasonably well acquainted with the words and idioms and phrases of colloquial language.

Another difficulty comes from the fact that in spoken English, as in all languages, people use many reduced forms. Reduction can be phonological ("Djedoit?" for "Did you do it?"), morphological (contractions like "I'll..."), syntactic (elliptical forms like the answer to "When is the paper due?" "Next Monday."), or pragmatic (The teacher asks a question, then points to a student in the classroom and says, "Tom! Please!"). These reductions pose significant difficulties, especially to classroom learners who may have only been exposed to the full forms of the English language.

Brown also mentions that the "prosodic features" of the English languages - stress, rhythm and intonation are very important for comprehension. As a "stress-timed" language, English can be a terror for some ESL learners as "mouthfuls of syllables come spilling out between stress points." (p.341) Also, intonation patterns are very significant not just for interpreting such straightforward elements as questions, statements and emphasis but more subtle messages like "sarcasm, endearment, insult, solicitation, praise, etc." (p. 341)

Some other reasons why listening to English as a foreign language is so challenging for ESL speakers are also suggested by Penny Ur (1988). First, when a foreigner is listening to someone speaking in English, he has to learn to deal with a certain amount of 'noise'. For example, in many natural settings "some words may be drowned by outside interference, others indistinctly pronounced" (p.13); so it becomes harder for a non-native English speaker to get the meaning of one's speaking. Second, some foreign language learners try to understand every single word of incoming speech, but actually, doing so is both unnecessary and impossible. It is not even advisable because when they are trying hard to get every individual word or phrase, listeners are not seeing "the forest for the trees." Third, "fatigue" negatively influences a foreign language learner's listening to English. In academic listening especially, the listener will feel tired trying to "understand the unfamiliar sounds, lexis and syntax for long stretches of time". Fourth, many foreign learners have difficulties in understanding different accents, because they have got used to the accent of their own teachers and they are usually "surprised and dismayed when they find they have difficulty understanding someone else" (p. 17).

CESL students experience special difficulties in listening to English lectures because of the great differences between Chinese and English, which are two non-cognate languages. The following are just some differences between Chinese and English mentioned by Li and Thompson (1981). First, unlike English, Chinese has very little morphological complexity. Generally, each Chinese word consists of just one morpheme and cannot be further analyzed into component parts. In English, speakers often mark nouns for a singular / plural distinction (*book/books*). But in Chinese speakers do not need to mark it. For example, *laoshi* can refer to either 'teacher' or 'teachers' in Chinese. Second, Chinese has no markers for tense, though it does have such aspect morphemes as *-le* (perfective), *-guo* (experienced action), etc. This accounts for CESL students' confusion in understanding various tenses in English. Third, in Chinese there is little inflectional grammar such as articles, verb conjugations, agreement between subject and predicate, etc. All these differences can cause special challenges for CESL students in understanding spoken English in class.

ABOUT THIS STUDY

To discover CESL students' academic listening problems at an American university and arrive at their solutions, the following research questions guided this study: a) What are the specific challenges that result from the English language for CESL students in understanding academic lectures at an American university? b) What are the specific non-linguistic challenges for CESL students in comprehending academic lectures? c) How do these challenges affect different types of CESL students? d) What is the main source of their challenges: linguistic or non-linguistic? And e) Given the answers to questions a, b, c, and d above, how can CESL students' academic listening skills be improved?

The subjects of this study were 78 full-time Mainland CESL students who enrolled in the 2000 winter semester at an American university. Among them, 46% are students of Arts and 54% are students of Science. About 77% of them are graduate students and 23% are undergraduates. About 72% of the participants have been in the United States for more than one year, and 28% are in their first year of study in the US. The subjects were asked to complete a questionnaire that consisted of a total number of 30 items and an open-ended question. Six out of the 30 items focused on the North American professors' use of English and its influence on CESL students' English academic listening. Most of the 30 items on the questionnaire required the subjects to mark their responses on a five-point Likert scale. The researcher used different data analysis methods such as descriptive statistics (frequencies and percentages), Factorial ANOVA and Chi-square to analyze the data. In the data analysis process, the subjects were categorized as the following four variables: a) gender (male/female), b) major (arts/science), c) status (undergraduate/graduate), and d) length of time studying in America (less than one year/more than one year). It was anticipated that there might be significant differences in CESL students' academic listening difficulties according to the above four variables.

RESULTS AND DISCUSSION

The results of this study reveal that both linguistic and non-linguistic factors jointly affect CESL students' comprehension of English academic lectures. Linguistic challenges are those that result from the English language itself. They are caused by both CESL students' lack of English proficiency and their American professors' use of English in class. Results of non-linguistic factors are addressed in Chapter Ten.

This chapter focuses on how American professors' use of English in class affects CESL students' English academic listening. Table 9.1 shows that a) the rapidness of professors' English speech; b) professors' lack of clear pronunciation; c) professors' use of long and complex sentences; d) professors' use of colloquial and slang expressions; e) professors' lack of clear definition of terms and concepts; and f) professors' use of discourse markers affect CESL students' English academic listening at an American university.

**Table 9.1. American Professors' Use of English Affects CESL Students'
Academic Listening**

Professors' Use of English	Number of Responses	Mean (Average Score)	Standard Deviation	Significant Differences	
Rapidness of speech	78	3.62	1.11	③	④
Lack of clear pronunciation	78	3.29	1.22	③	
Use of long/complex sentences	78	3.17	1.32	②	③
Use of colloquial/slang expressions	78	3.44	1.29	②	③
Lack of clear definition of terms/concepts	78	3.39	1.06	③	④
Use of discourse markers	78	3.78	0.89	②	③

* The 5-point Likert Scale responses range from point 1 (strongly disagree/very negatively) to point 5 (strongly agree/very positively).   ① Gender   ② Major   ③ Status   ④ Length of time studying in America

THE EFFECTS OF RAPIDNESS OF AMERICAN TEACHERS' SPEECH ON LECTURE COMPREHENSION

When Chinese students were learning English in China, the great majority did not have native speakers as their English teachers. So they did not familiarize themselves with the normal or natural speed of native speakers' English speaking. For this reason they might think that all the American teachers were speaking English too fast. This question was intended to investigate to what degree the rapidness of American teachers' speech affected students' lecture comprehension. The question read as follows: "Does the rapidness of your American teachers' speech affect your comprehension of a lecture (1 = not at all 5 = very much)?"

The results of this question show that only 19.2% of the subjects chose scale points 1 and 2, which means that relatively few subjects did not think the rapidness of their American teachers' speech affected their comprehension of a lecture very much. On the other hand, 53.8% of them chose scale points 4 and 5. This response pattern indicates that the great majority had difficulty in understanding a lecture because their American teachers were speaking too fast in class.

The Factorial ANOVA showed statistically significant differences ($p < .01$) in participants' responses to this question between: undergraduate students and graduate students, 1- (studying time in US < one year) students and 1+ (studying time in US > one year) students. The results of the *post hoc* analysis for this question showed that undergraduates (mean = 4.50) reported more frequently than graduate students (mean = 3.35) that the rapidness of their American teachers speech affected their understanding of a lecture. Similarly, more 1- students (mean = 4.05) indicated that the rapidness of their American teachers' speech caused more challenges for them in understanding a lecture than the 1+ students (mean = 3.45). This was probably because they had not become used to their

American teachers' speed of speech. When they were in China, they did not have native speakers as their English teachers.

THE EFFECTS OF LACK OF CLEAR PRONUNCIATION ON LECTURE COMPREHENSION

Because CESL students were used to their Chinese English teachers' slow and clear pronunciation, they apparently had problems in understanding native speakers' English. The question read as follows: "I have difficulty in understanding a lecture because my American teachers do not usually pronounce each word clearly in class (1 = strongly disagree 5 = strongly agree)."

Results show that the largest number of the subjects chose the middle response. Just 28.2% of the subjects (scale points 1 and 2) thought that the lack of their American teachers' clear pronunciation of each word did not cause much difficulty for them in understanding a lecture. On the other hand, 44.9% of them chose responses 4 and 5, indicating that their American teachers' pronunciation made it difficult for them to understand a lecture.

The Factorial ANOVA showed statistically significant differences in participants' responses to this question between undergraduate students and graduate students ($p < .01$). There was no difference between the groups on the other three independent variables. The results of the *post hoc* analysis for this question showed that there was a significant difference between undergraduate (mean = 4.50) and graduate students (mean = 2.93) in the responses to this question. This is probably because undergraduate students had less general academic experience than graduate students or the graduate classes themselves were probably smaller in size, different from the undergraduate classes.

THE EFFECTS OF TEACHERS' USE OF LONG AND COMPLEX SENTENCES ON LECTURE COMPREHENSION

In addition to the natural rapidness of their speech and their unclear pronunciation, some American teachers use many long and complex sentences when delivering lectures. The use of long and complex sentences can make it hard for non-native speakers to understand a lecture. The following question asked about the effects of long and complex sentences on lecture comprehension. It read as follows: "My teachers' use of long and complex sentences makes it hard for me to understand a lecture (1 = strongly disagree 5 = strongly agree)."

The results show that about 35.9% of the subjects (scale points 1 and 2) thought that their teachers' use of long and complex sentences did not make it hard for them to understand a lecture. But 43.6% of them (scale points 4 and 5) agreed that the use of long and complex sentences did cause them problems in understanding a lecture. Long and complex sentences contain complicated structures and more information. They may create challenges for non-native speakers in understanding a lecture. If the students are not familiar with the topic and background information, or they do not possess a certain amount of required vocabulary, they may feel even more difficult to understand these long and complex sentences.

The results of the statistical analysis for this question showed statistically significant differences ($p < .01$) in participants' responses to this question between: undergraduate students (mean = 4.50) and graduate students (mean = 2.78), arts students (mean = 3.56) and science students (mean = 2.83).

THE EFFECTS OF COLLOQUIAL AND SLANG EXPRESSSIONS ON LECTURE COMPREHENSION

As previously discussed, colloquial and slang expressions are likely to cause problems for non-native speakers in understanding a lecture. The following question asked about the effects of the teachers' use of colloquial and slang expressions on CESL students' lecture comprehension. It read as follows: "My teachers use a lot of colloquial and slang expressions in class, which makes it difficult for me to understand the lecture (1 = strongly disagree 5 = strongly agree)."

The results of this question show that 50.1% of the subjects (scale points 4 and 5) agreed that their teachers' use of colloquial and slang expressions made it hard for them to comprehend a lecture, while only 24.3% of the subjects (scale points 1 and 2) disagreed with this statement.

The results of the ANOVA analysis showed statistically significant differences ($p < .01$) in participants' responses to this question between undergraduate students (mean = 4.22) and graduate students (mean = 3.20), and arts students (mean = 4.06) and science students (mean = 2.90). The results indicate that undergraduate students had more problems with colloquial and slang expressions than graduate students. This was probably because undergraduate students had less academic experience with colloquial or slang expressions or they lacked that type of vocabulary. Similarly, arts students had more problems with colloquial and slang expressions than science students. This was probably because arts teachers used more colloquial and slang expressions than science teachers because of the different nature of arts lectures.

THE EFFECTS OF LACK OF CLEAR DEFINITIONS ON LECTURE COMPREHENSION

Clear definitions of some important terms and concepts provided by the teachers might help their students better understand a lecture. The following question asked about the effects of lack of clear definitions on lecture comprehension. It read as follows: "My teachers do not always provide students with a clear definition of some terms and important concepts, which creates lecture comprehension problems (1 = strongly disagree 5 = strongly agree)."

The results show that 47.5% of the subjects (scale points 4 and 5) reported that they could not fully understand a class lecture because their American teachers did not always provide them with clear definitions of some terms and important concepts. Less than half that number, only 21.7% of them (scale point 1 and 2) did not think that was true. Some important terms and new concepts could be the important part of a lecture. The failure to explain them clearly could make it very hard for students to understand a lecture.

The Factorial ANOVA showed statistically significant differences ($p < .01$) in participants' responses to this question between: undergraduate students and graduate students, 1- students and 1+ students. Their American professors' failure to provide clear definitions of some terms and important concepts caused more problems for undergraduate students (mean = 4.11) than graduate students (mean = 3.15). Similarly, 1- students (mean = 3.86) reported they had more challenges on that than 1+ students (mean = 3.18). This was probably because graduate students and 1+ students had more learning experience and knowledge and they could understand these terms and concepts better than undergraduate students and 1- students.

THE EFFECTS OF DISCOURSE ON LECTURE COMPREHENSION

As previously discussed, discourse markers such as *well, OK, so, now* can help students better understand a class lecture. The following question was intended to investigate the effects of discourse markers on lecture comprehension: "The teacher uses a lot of signals such as *well, OK, so, now*. Does the use of these signals affect your comprehension of a lecture positively or negatively (1 = very negatively, 5 = very positively)?"

The results show that 60.3% of the subjects (scale points 4 and 5) agreed that their American teachers' use of signal words or discourse markers helped them understand a class lecture. Some subjects commented that signal words indicated the sequence or direction of a lecture and they could lead them to a better or fuller understanding of a class lecture. On the other hand, only 6.4% of them (scale point 2), a very tiny minority, reported that the use of signal words created challenges in comprehending a lecture.

The results of the ANOVA analysis for this question also show statistically significant differences in participants' responses to this question between: undergraduate students and graduate students ($p < .01$), arts students and science students ($p < .05$). These results tell us that undergraduate students (mean = 4.33) and arts students (mean = 4.22) realized the usefulness or help of signal words in understanding a lecture better than graduate students (mean = 3.62) and science students (mean = 3.40).

CESL STUDENTS' SUGGESTIONS FOR THEIR AMERICAN PROFESSOR

In terms of professors' use of English CESL students made some practical suggestions for their American professors in response to the open-ended question. The following are some selected suggestions for American professors:

1. The teacher can speak a little more slowly when delivering a lecture.
2. The teacher should use formal English to deliver lectures.
3. The teacher should avoid using colloquial and slang expressions.
4. The teacher should explain some important concepts clearly in class.
5. The teacher should vary the pace of lesson and break up content into accessible units.

6. The teacher should speak clearly and loudly in the classroom.
7. The teacher should try to get rid of strong accent and strange pronunciation.
8. The teacher should use more body language to facilitate students' learning.

In total, 20 suggestions were raised for American teachers. Arts students offered more suggestions for their American professors than science students. This is probably because arts students had more linguistic challenges than science students in understanding English academic lectures. Thirty-four participants (44%) suggested that American professors use formal and easy-to-understand English in order to make their lectures more accessible to CESL students and other international students. For example, they might slow down their speech, pronounce more distinctly, explain or define unfamiliar words, carefully plan and explain examples to be used. Most suggestions for American professors required them to be aware of the non-native English students in their classes and try to help them learn more effectively.

CONCLUSION

The study[1] showed that American professors' use of English affects CESL students' English academic listening at an American university. First, American teachers' English speech characteristics create some challenges. About 53.8% of the subjects report having problems in understanding English lectures because their American teachers speak English quickly in class. About 44.9% of the subjects experience difficulty in understanding lectures because their American teachers do not pronounce each word clearly.

Second, American teachers' use of long and complex sentences creates challenges. About 43.6% of the subjects report having challenges in understanding lectures because their American teachers use long and complex sentences.

Third, American teachers' use of colloquial and slang expressions makes it difficult for CESL students to understand English lectures. More than half of the subjects report experiencing this challenge and most of them are arts students. This is probably because arts teachers use more colloquial and slang expressions than science teachers.

Fourth, 47.5% of the subjects report they cannot fully understand a class lecture because their American teachers do not always provide them with clear definitions of some terms and important concepts.

Fifth, about 60% of the CESL students report that their American teachers' use of signal words (discourse markers) help them to understand a lecture. The results show that arts students realize the usefulness of the discourse markers better than science students.

Finally, arts students report they are experiencing more linguistic challenges than science students. They express difficulty in understanding English lectures because their American teachers use difficult vocabulary and expressions and complex structures. This is probably true because science students already know the basic science vocabularies in Chinese, because Chinese borrows heavily from English in scientific and technical language, but not in arts disciplines. In mathematics and chemistry classes, teachers use the same formulas in both English and Chinese. All these factors can help science students better understand a lecture.

---

[1] This article was originally published in *College Student Journal*.

REFERENCES

Algier W. (Eds.), *Improving Reading and Study Skills*. San Francisco: Jossey-Bass.

Anderson-Mejias, P. L. (1986). English for academic listening: Teaching the skills associated with listening to extended discourse. *Foreign Language Annals, 19,* 391-398.

Brown, H. D. (1994). *Teaching by principles.* New Jersey: Prentice Hall Agents. Chaudron, C., and Richards, J. C. (1985). *The effect of discourse markers on the comprehension of lectures.* Paper presented at the 19th Annual Convention of TESOL, New York.

Conaway, M. (1982). Listening: Learning too and retention agent. In A. S. Algier and K.

Ferris D., and Tagg, T. (1996). Academic listening/speaking tasks for ESL students: Problems, suggestions, and implications. *TESOL Quarterly, 30,* 297-317.

Flowerdew, J. (1995). Research of relevance to second language lecture comprehension: An overview. In J. Flowerdew (Ed.), *Academic listening: Research perspectives* (pp7-29). Cambridge: Cambridge University Press.

Flowerdew, J., and Miller, L. (1997). The teaching of academic listening and the question of authenticity. *English for Special Purposes 16,* 27-46.

Institute of International Education. (2000, May 16). *98/99 opendoors on the Web.*[Selections from the book], New York. Retrieved June 15, 2000 from the World Wide Web: http://www.opendoorsweb.org/Lead%20Stories/international_studs.htm

Li, C. N., and Thompson, S. A. (1981). *Mandarin Chinese: A functional reference grammar.* Los Angeles: University of California Press.

Murphy, D. F., and Candlin. C. N. (1979). Engineering lecture discourse and listening comprehension. *Practical Papers in Language Education, 2,* 1-79. Lancaster, England: University of Lancaster.

Powers, D. (1985). A survey of academic demands related to listening skills. (TOEFL Research Report No. 20). Princeton, NJ: Educational Testing Service.

Richards, J. (1983). Listening comprehension: Approach, design, procedure. *TESOL Quarterly, 17,* 219-239.

Ur, P. (1988). *Teaching listening comprehension.* Cambridge: Cambridge University Press.

Yuan, D. Z. (1982). *Chinese scientists' difficulties in comprehending English science lectures.* M.A. in TESL thesis, University of California at Los Angles, Los Angles.

In: East Meets West
Editor: Jinyan Huang

ISBN: 978-1-62618-195-3
© 2013 Nova Science Publishers, Inc.

Chapter 10

NORTH AMERICAN PROFESSORS' TEACHING STYLES AFFECT CHINESE ESL STUDENTS' ACADEMIC LISTENING

Jinyan Huang[1]* and Shuangli Su[2]
[1]Niagara University, Lewiston, New York, US
[2]Untested Ideas Research Center, Niagara Falls, New York, US

ABSTRACT

Academic listening plays an important role in an ESL university student's academic success. Research has begun to show that ESL students have difficulty in English academic listening at American universities. Chinese ESL (CESL) students, who are from a different educational system and cultural environment, experience particular challenges in English academic listening. This study focuses on their challenges as reported by CESL students in understanding English lectures. Seventy-eight CESL students at an American university were asked to complete a questionnaire that consisted of 30 items and an open-ended question. Most of the items required them to mark their responses on a five-point Likert scale. This chapter focuses on American classroom instructional factors that CESL students report affect their English academic listening. CESL students report that the following instructional factors affect their English academic listening at an American university: a) lecture organization, b) use of textbooks, c) blackboard writing, d) lecture summary, e) amount of student participation, and f) amount of group work. The chapter offers suggestions for American professors about how to make their lectures more accessible to CESL students.

INTRODUCTION

Listening has been regarded as the most frequently used language skill in the classroom. It plays an even more important role in one's academic success than reading skill or academic

---

* Correspondence concerning this chapter should be addressed to Dr. Jinyan Huang at *jhuang@niagara.edu*.

aptitude (Conaway, 1982). Research shows that ESL students have difficulty understanding academic lectures at American universities. Chinese ESL (CESL) students, who are from a different educational system and cultural environment, experience particular challenges in understanding academic lectures in English. The question of which factors affect their academic lecture comprehension merits closer examination. Recognizing their challenges in understanding English lectures is the first step; the next is to discover the sources of these challenges and to propose solutions. This chapter reports the sources and suggests solutions to challenges of academic listening as reported by CESL students at an American university.

THEORETICAL BACKGROUND

Academic Listening: Definition and Importance

Listening purposes vary according to whether learners or not are involved in listening as a component of social interaction. Brown and Yule (1983) classified listening functions or purposes as interactional and transactional. The purpose of interactional listening is to engage in social interaction. Participants usually make these interactions "comfortable and non-threatening" and their purpose is to communicate "good will" (Richards, 1994).

In contrast, the purpose of transactional listening is primarily to communicate information. Accurate and coherent communication of the message is required. It is important for the listener to get the direct and exact meaning of the message in transactional listening. For example, news broadcasts, lectures, descriptions, and instructions are all transactional uses of language (Richards, 1994). "Speakers typically go to considerable trouble to make what they are saying clear when a transaction is involved, and may contradict the listener if he appears to have misunderstood." (Brown and Yule, 1983, p.13)

Transactional listening is common in academic listening. Academic listening involves listening and speaking tasks in university classes. According to Flowerdew (1995), it has its own characteristics and places special demands upon listeners. To be a successful academic listener, a student needs relevant background knowledge, the ability to distinguish between important and unimportant information, and appropriate skills like note taking. Richards (1983) also suggests many micro-skills are required for academic listening: the ability to identify the purpose and scope of a lecture, the ability to identify the topic of a lecture and follow topic development, the ability to identify the role of discourse markers in signaling the structure of a lecture (p. 229).

Academic listening plays a crucial role in a student's academic success. In a study by Powers (1985), American and Canadian professors of engineering, psychology, chemistry, computer science, English, and business rated listening and speaking highest when asked to give the relative importance of listening, speaking, reading, and writing for international students' success in their academic departments.

Educational research has indicated that native speakers of English often have trouble comprehending university lectures (Brown, 1998). Research in English for Academic Purposes (EAP) has begun to show that ESL students have great difficulty in understanding academic lectures at American universities. Ferris and Tagg (1996) investigated university professors' views on ESL students' difficulties with listening tasks. Instructors at four different institutions and in a variety of academic disciplines responded to questions and provided comments about their ESL students' listening skills. All respondents reported that their ESL students had great difficulty with lecture comprehension, responding to questions, and class participation.

Among the ESL learners in American universities, CESL students are the largest group. Data show that the two world regions sending the largest proportions of students to the US are Asia and Latin America, and students from China are the largest single group (Open Doors, 2001). Investigating factors that affect CESL students' challenges of academic listening in English has important educational implications for American university educators.

Learning in Different Cultural Contexts

Academic listening is one component of academic learning. Tweed and Lehman (2002) argued that academic learning varies depending on the cultural context. A Confucian-Socratic framework was used to analyze the influence of different cultural contexts on academic learning. In this framework, Socratic-oriented learning involves "overt and private questioning, expression of personal hypotheses, and a desire for self-directed tasks" (p. 93). Confucian-oriented learning involves "effort-focused conceptions of learning, pragmatic orientations to learning, and acceptance of behavioral reform as an academic goal" (p. 93).

Socrates (469-399 BC), a Western exemplar, valued the questioning of both his own and others' beliefs, the evaluation of others' knowledge, self-generated knowledge, and teaching by implanting doubt. Confucius (551-479 BC), an Eastern exemplar, valued effortful learning, respectful learning, and pragmatic acquisition of essential knowledge (Tweed and Lehman, 2002).

Confucius' philosophy has a strong impact on Chinese people's viewpoints, ways of thinking, and behaviors. His philosophy of learning can be summarized as "effortful learning, behavioral reform, pragmatic learning, acquisition of essential knowledge, and respectful learning" (Tweed and Lehman, 2002, p. 91). Confucius stressed the importance of hard work. He believed that one's success came mainly from his/her hard work not his/her ability. He also believed that "behavior reform is a central goal of education because virtuous behavior can ensure individual success and societal harmony" (p. 92). Confucius valued pragmatic learning. He viewed the goal of learning as to competently conduct oneself within a civil service job. He stressed the acquisition of essential knowledge and respectful learning. He taught his students to respect and obey authorities. He once said that "to honor those higher than ourselves is the highest expression of the sense of justice" (p. 332). When they come to American universities, many CESL students bring a Confucian-oriented perspective to their learning, while their professors may have a more Socratic orientation.

Distinct Characteristics of Academic Listening

Academic listening has distinct characteristics and places high demands upon listeners (Flowerdew, 1995). It requires listeners to have relevant background information on the lecture delivered. It also requires listeners to be able to distinguish between what is relevant and what is not relevant because an academic lecture contains both relevant and irrelevant information on the topic discussed. Academic listening contains long stretches of talk when listeners do not have the opportunity to engage in the facilitating functions of interactive discourse, so it places high demands upon listeners.

In their empirical research, Flowerdew and Miller (1997) described some additional features that differentiate authentic lecture discourse from written text or scripted lectures. An authentic lecture is often structured according to "tone groups" and in the form of incomplete clauses. It is often signaled by "micro-level discourse markers" such as "and," "so," "but," "now," "okay." What's more, in an authentic lecture, speakers use many false starts, hesitations, corrections, and repetitions. Speakers often organize their thoughts poorly and present their ideas in complete grammatical sentences. This makes it difficult for the listeners to understand the information delivered in the lecture.

Finally, Ferris and Tagg (1996) comment that there is frequent "give" and "take" between teacher and students in an academic classroom situation. This includes formal, planned lecture material, informal questions or comments from the students, and unplanned responses to students by the professor. During these give-and-take activities, students become more involved. On the one hand, they have to actively participate in these activities; on the other hand they have to comprehend what is going on in class and try to get the important points of the lecture. So understanding lectures poses formidable challenges for ESL students, even those highly proficient in English.

Effects of Lecture Organization on Academic Listening

Academic listening comprehension is often difficult for ESL students for many reasons. First, their difficulties come from the English language itself. English creates challenges for them (Brown, 1994). For example, a new word, an unfamiliar pronunciation, or a complex sentence structure can cause challenges for them in understanding an English lecture. Second, there are obvious difficulties for non-native speakers in understanding academic lectures. Benson (1989) identified the following difficulties in a case study: the new content, the unfamiliar background, and the American lecture format. Third, ESL learners have challenges in understanding academic lectures because they do not have the appropriate learning strategies or skills. Ferris and Tagg (1996) concluded in their survey study that ESL learners' difficulty would be reduced if they had effective learning strategies and good preparation for the subject-matter lectures in EAP classes.

The organization of academic lectures is an important factor that affects ESL learners' comprehension. In a study of lecture transcript analysis, Lebauer (1984) commented that many non-native English-speaking students, who are not aware of the standard organization of an academic lecture or the conventions and cues which signal important information in lectures delivered in a foreign language, face problems in academic lecture comprehension.

The purpose of academic lectures is to teach content matter, and to have information presented, understood, and remembered. The structuring or organizing of a lecture is an essential aspect of its comprehensibility (Chaudron and Richards, 1986). Cook (1975) describes the "macro-structure" of a lecture as being composed of a number of "expositions."

These consist of an optional episode of expectation, an obligatory focal episode, an obligatory developmental episode together with optional developmental episodes, and an obligatory closing episode. At the level of micro-structure, episodes are described in terms of moves. For example, a concluding move is a justificatory statement, a focal episode with a concluding function, or a summary statement.

Diamond, Sharp and Ory (1983) suggest that effective lecture preparation and delivery can be arranged under the following three stages: 1) the beginning; 2) the body; and 3) the closing. In the beginning stage, the lecturer usually relates lecture content to previous class material, mentions the background of the current lecture, or gives students a brief introduction of the content of the current lecture. In the body of the lecture, there is some flexibility for the lecturer to present the content. The lecturer can either decide the main points and explain them clearly to the listeners or organize the material in some logical order such as "cause-effect," "time-sequential," etc. During the lecture the lecturer may ask questions to check on students' understanding of the lecture or ask them to make their comments. In the last stage of the lecture, the lecturer may briefly summarize the content of the lecture or reemphasize what he or she expects students to learn from the lecture.

Therefore, if students have some knowledge about the organization of an academic lecture and they are familiar with different stages of a lecture, they may be better able to infer relationships between different sections and gain a solid understanding of the content.

CESL Students in American Classrooms

CESL students often feel uncomfortable with the students' behavior in American classrooms. Upton (1989) argues that CESL students at American universities have a negative reaction toward American students' behavior. Students are late for class. They may ask the teacher questions or make jokes in class. All these behaviors are considered rude and disrespectful in Chinese classrooms. In American classrooms students can challenge their professors at any time by interrupting them and asking them questions, which makes CESL students feel that students do not show any respect for their professors.

Chen (1985) also reports that CESL students do not feel comfortable with American students' self-centeredness. Students come to the classroom as individuals, may study whatever subjects they are really in and not care what other people think of them. After class, they may pay no attention to what their fellow students are doing. In China, students care what the teacher and other students think of them. If students cannot correctly answer the teachers' questions in class, they think that they have "lost face" and feel embarrassed and even ashamed. They are often afraid of making mistakes (Ma and Huang, 1992).

America and China have different cultures and traditions. The roles of the teacher, for example, are defined and interpreted differently. Fu (1991) argues that in Chinese culture there is lack of the spirit of equality in the classrooms. Teachers are regarded not only as authorities in their field of study but also as students' moral mentor. But in American classrooms, there is a more equal relationship between teachers and students. While Chinese teachers are always serious and focus on lecturing, American teachers often use humor and varied, informal teaching methods in the classroom. Differences in teaching style comprise a significant cultural difference for CESL students (Upton, 1989).

ABOUT THE STUDY

Research Questions

To date, some studies have been conducted on CESL students' general academic learning challenges at American universities (Chen, 1999; Feng, 1991; Sun and Chen, 1997; Zhong, 1996). Little research, however, has been conducted on the factors that affect their English academic listening. To contribute to understanding CESL students' academic listening problems at American universities and to recommend solutions, the following research questions guided this study: a) What are the specific challenges that CESL students report result from the English language in their understanding academic lectures at an American university? b) What are the specific non-linguistic challenges reported by CESL students in comprehending academic lectures? c) How do different types of CESL students report these challenges that affect them? d) What is the main source of their challenges: linguistic or non-linguistic? And e) Given the answers to questions a, b, c, and d above, what do CESL students suggest would improve their academic listening?

Participants

The participants of this study were 78 full-time Mainland CESL students who were enrolled during the 2000 winter semester at an American university. Among them, 46% are students of Arts, and 54% are students of Science. About 77% are graduate students, and 23% are undergraduates. About 72% of the participants have been in the United States for more than one year, and 28% are in their first year of study in the US.

Instrument

A questionnaire was used to elicit the CESL students' frank opinions concerning what their difficulties in understanding English lectures at an American university were and what suggestions they would raise for both themselves and their American professors. In order to collect more accurate data, the questionnaire was translated into Chinese before data collection procedures. The questionnaire consisted of three parts. The first part collected personal, demographic information including gender, major, years at the school, years in the US, and TOEFL scores.

The second part consisted of two sections, each of which dealt with one of the sources of CESL students' English academic listening challenges (linguistic and non-linguistic). The total number of items in this part was 30, and item types varied. Under each item space was provided for the participants to make additional comments. Twenty-five items required the CESL students to mark their responses on a five-point Likert scale; three items required them to rank order categories; two were multiple-choice questions; and the final item asked the participants to choose one main source (either linguistic or non-linguistic) of their challenges in understanding English academic lectures. Six of the 30 items focused on the American professors' instructional methodology and its effects on CESL students' English academic listening, and all of the six items were on a five-point Likert scale (see Appendix A). These items were included because the researcher believed that CESL students had different classroom learning experience in China, and the American instructional methodology might cause problems for them in understanding English academic lectures.

The third part was an open-ended question. The participants of this study were asked to give suggestions, for both themselves and their American teachers, of solutions to their academic listening problems.

Data Analysis

The data obtained for each item were first analyzed by using descriptive statistical methods. For the 25 five-point scale items, the percentage of responses for each point on the scale was calculated. Then the mean score and standard deviation for each item were calculated. A Factorial ANOVA was also used to determine whether there was a significant difference in the responses according to the following 4 independent variables: a) gender (male/female), b) major (arts/science), c) level of study (undergraduate/graduate), and d) length of time studying in America (less than one year/more than one year). If there were significant differences between the independent variables, a descriptive *post hoc* analysis was conducted to see where the differences occurred.

For the ranking items, the percentage of respondents choosing each point on the scale was calculated. Then the standard deviation and mean score of each item were calculated by assigning eight points to the top ranked item, seven points to the second place, six points to the third place, etc., in the case of the eight-point items.

For the last item, which asked CESL students to choose one main source (either linguistic or non-linguistic) of their challenges in understanding English lectures, four *Chi*-square tests were used to see if there was a statistically significant difference ($p < .05$) between two groups in each of the above-mentioned 4 independent variables.

For the open-ended question, every response was categorized into groups of similar responses, and categories placed in a frequency order with most frequent at the top. In order to increase the inter-rater reliability, two colleagues of the researcher were invited to categorize all the participants' responses to the open-ended question. Most of the subjects answered the open-ended question in Chinese. The three raters first carefully read all the responses and translated the Chinese responses into English. After that they worked individually to put the similar responses together to form a suggestion.

RESULTS AND DISCUSSION

The results of this study revealed that both linguistic and non-linguistic factors were reported to affect CESL students' comprehension of English academic lectures. Non-linguistic factors included instructional, psychological, and individual factors. Results of reports of effects of linguistic factors have been addressed in Chapter Nine.

**Table 10.1. American Instructional Factors Affecting CESL Students'
Academic Listening**

Instructional Factors and Effects	Number of Responses	Mean	Standard Deviation	Significant Differences ($p < .05$)
Effects of lecture organization	78	3.63	1.20	② ③
Use of Textbooks and its effects	78	3.55	1.15	②
	78	4.03	1.02	③
Blackboard writing and its effects	78	3.67	1.03	③ ②
	78	3.97	1.14	②
Lecture summary and its effects	78	3.89	1.02	③ ②
	78	4.08	1.05	③
Amount of student participation and its effects	78	1.92	1.11	②
	78	4.04	1.13	②
Amount of group work and its effects	78	2.00	1.07	②
	78	3.87	1.02	② ③

Note: ① Gender   ② Major   ③ Level of study   ④ Length of time studying in America

This chapter focuses on how instructional factors affected CESL students' English academic listening as reported by CESL students. Table 10.1 shows that CESL students report a) lecture organization, b) use of textbooks, c) blackboard writing, d) lecture summary, e) amount of student participation, and f) amount of group work affect their academic listening at an American university.

The Effects of Lecture Organization on Lecture Comprehension

Item # 14 on the questionnaire asked about the effects of lecture organization on lecture comprehension (see Appendix A). The organizing of a lecture is an essential aspect of its comprehensibility and good lecture organization could help students; especially ESL students better understand it (Chaudron and Richards, 1986; Diamond, Sharp and Ory, 1983).

The results show that 60.3% of the participants agreed that their American teachers' organization of a lecture affected their understanding of it. In the comment area under the question, some participants commented that their American teachers did not logically organize their lectures and CESL students expected their teachers to make everything clear for them, including the difficult points and the important points. On the other hand, only 20.5% of the participants reported that their American teachers' lecture organization did not affect their lecture comprehension.

The results also show statistically significant difference by major and level of study. There was no significant difference by gender and by length of time studying in America. Undergraduate students (mean = 4.39) reported that their American professors' organization of a lecture had more effects on their comprehension than graduate students (mean = 3.40) did. Similar differences were found between arts students (mean = 4.03) and science students (mean = 3.29). Different comments made by arts students and science students might explain the differences. Arts lectures are usually less focused and not well organized. Science professors normally use a straightforward way to organize their lectures.

The Effects of Using Textbooks on Lecture Comprehension

In Chinese culture, textbooks have authority over teachers (Fu, 1991). Teachers always closely follow the textbook while lecturing. The teachers go into details about each chapter of the textbook through each term. While in America, teachers do not feel constrained to follow the textbook and the syllabus, and they do not "worry about getting sidetracked onto some tangential topic in the middle of a lecture" (Upton, 1989, p. 25) either. This difference in following the textbooks might cause some problems for CESL students in understanding an English lecture.

According to the results of Item # 15 (see Appendix A), 55.2% of the participants reported that their American teachers did not closely follow the textbooks while lecturing. On the other hand, 20.4% of them reported that their American teachers closely followed the textbook while lecturing. There was significant difference by major. Arts students (mean = 4.11) reported that most of their American teachers did not closely follow the textbook while lecturing. Science students (mean = 3.07) reported that their teachers usually followed the textbook while lecturing. There was no difference by the other three independent variables.

Among all the participants, 71.8% of them reported that American professors' failure to follow textbooks affected their lecture comprehension. There was significant difference by level of study. Undergraduate students (mean = 4.72) reported to have a stronger agreement that American teachers' use of textbooks affected their comprehension of lectures than graduate students (mean = 3.82). This was perhaps because graduate students have more academic learning experiences and stronger self-study skills than undergraduate students. There was no difference by the other three independent variables.

The Effects of Blackboard Writing on Lecture Comprehension

Item # 16 on the questionnaire (see Appendix A) was intended to uncover both American professors' general practice of blackboard writing and its effects on CESL students' comprehension of English lectures. Among all the participants, 56.5% of them reported that their American teachers did not write much on the board while lecturing; only 10.2% of them reported that their American teachers did write much on the board while lecturing, and all of them were science students. The results show significant differences by both level of study and major. There was no difference by major and length of time studying in America. Unlike graduate students (mean = 3.52) and science students (mean = 3.33), undergraduate students (mean = 4.17) and arts students (mean = 4.06) reported that their teachers almost did not write anything on the board while lecturing.

Among all the participants, 74.4% of them agreed that teachers' writing on the board affected their understanding of the lecture. The results show differences between arts students (mean = 4.72) and science students (mean = 3.78). Arts students reported to have a stronger agreement than science students that blackboard writing did affect lecture comprehension.

In Chinese universities, teachers write much on the blackboard while lecturing. They always put the important and difficult points on the blackboard. Blackboard writing can give students a deep impression and help them better understand a lecture (Ma and Huang, 1992). While at American universities, teachers, teachers of arts in particular, do not write much on the board while lecturing and the lack of blackboard writing causes problems for CESL students in understanding academic lectures. CESL students are used to point-by-point lectures with outlines and key points put on the blackboard. Upton (1989) mentioned that American university lectures are broad and extensive compared with the "intensive, narrow, and detailed" (p. 25) lectures in Chinese classrooms. CESL students often get confused about what they should learn about a lecture. Upton interviewed a CESL student and reported that:

"One Chinese student I interviewed said that she felt frustrated because she was not always sure what exactly the teachers wanted her to know. When she asked a teacher to help her out, his response of "You don't have to understand everything" really confused her (Upton, 1989, p. 25).

CESL students expect their American teachers to give detailed explanation of every topic and put the key points or outline on the blackboard in order for them to take detailed notes. When their expectations are not met, they intend to think that their American teachers are not so resourceful and responsible as their teachers back in China. But actually it is a question of academic learning in different cultural contexts. American teachers expect their students to do extensive reading and look for related information on their own outside of class (Upton, 1989).

The Effects of Lecture Summary on Lecture Comprehension

Chinese teachers usually summarize the main idea of a lecture at the end of it. Lecture summary can reemphasize the important points of a lecture (Diamond, Sharp and Ory, 1983). Item # 17 on the questionnaire (see Appendix A) was intended to uncover both American professors' general practice of using lecture summary and its effects on CESL students' comprehension of English lectures.

Among all the participants, 65.4% of the participants reported that their teachers did not usually summarize a lecture at the end of it. The results show differences by level of study and major. There was no difference by gender and length of time studying in America. Undergraduate (mean = 4.39) and arts (mean = 4.36) students have a stronger agreement than graduate (mean = 3.63) and science (mean = 3.45) students that their American professors do not usually give lecture summaries.

Almost 80% of the participants agreed that it did affect their lecture comprehension if American teachers failed to summarize the lecture at the end of it, because almost every teacher in Chinese universities does so and CESL students had the same expectations for lectures in their American classes. The results also show significant difference by level of study. Undergraduate students (mean = 4.78) reported that they had more problems in lecture comprehension than graduate students (mean = 3.87) if the teacher failed to give lecture summaries. There was no difference by the other three independent variables.

The Effects of Amount of Student Participation on Lecture Comprehension

According to the results of Item # 20 (see Appendix A), 76.9% of the participants reported that there was usually much student participation in class. The results show significant differences by major. Arts students (mean = 1.31) reported there was more student participation in their classrooms than in science classrooms (mean = 2.40). There was no difference on the other three independent variables.

More than 71% of the participants also reported that student participation affected their understanding of English academic lectures. This is probably because CESL students used to work individually in Chinese classrooms and they have not quite become used to participating in American classrooms. There was significant difference by major. Arts students (mean = 4.39) reported to have a stronger agreement than science students (mean = 3.74) that student participation did affect their comprehension of class lectures at an American university. There was no difference by the other three independent variables in terms of the effects of student participation on lecture comprehension.

The Effects of Amount of Group Work on Lecture Comprehension

Item # 22 on the questionnaire was intended to both the amount of group work in American classrooms and its effects on CESL students' academic lecture understanding (see Appendix A). 74.4% of the participants reported that there was much group work or class discussion in their classes. There was significant difference by major. Arts students (mean = 1.44) reported that there is more group work or class discussion in arts classes than science students (mean = 2.48) reported in science classes. There was no difference by the other three variables.

As many as 62.8% of the participants reported that the amount of group work or class discussion affected their understanding of English academic lectures. The results show statistically significant differences by major and level of study. Undergraduate (mean = 4.56) and arts (mean = 4.33) students reported to have a stronger agreement than graduate (mean = 3.67) and science (mean = 3.48) students that the amount of group work did affect lecture comprehension. There was no significant difference by gender and length of time studying in America.

Some participants made the following comments. In Chinese classrooms, students tend to work individually due to various reasons: class size (too many students in one classroom), the traditional role of a student (uncomfortable feeling of participating), and psychological impact (being afraid of making mistakes and losing face). Chinese teachers are usually explainers, and Chinese students act as listeners and note takers. There is not much group work or discussion in Chinese classrooms. Therefore, many CESL students feel difficult in adapting themselves to American classroom culture.

American teachers usually regard themselves as students' facilitators of learning but not their authorities of knowledge. They can admit their ignorance on a topic. Generally they do not easily get angry by students' challenging questions as Chinese teachers do. They give students' freedom in expressing their different ideas. They do not directly give answers to a particular question. What they stress is students' thinking and discussion. Therefore, they encourage students to be active in classroom discussions and praise critical and daring ideas

(Upton, 1989). This is the reason why in American classrooms there is much group work or discussion.

CESL STUDENTS' SUGGESTIONS FOR AMERICAN PROFESSORS

In response to the open-ended question (see Appendix A), CESL students made the following practical suggestions for their American professors to consider the modification or adjustment of their teaching methodologies:

1. American teachers should write key words, phrases, and ideas on the chalkboard in class.
2. The teacher should closely follow the textbook. If the teacher is teaching something not related to the textbook, he/she should provide students with related materials in advance.
3. The teacher can either put main points of a lecture on the web site or give us a copy of the main points so that we don't have to spend much time taking notes in class.
4. The teacher should often encourage international students to actively participate in class lectures.
5. The teacher should be aware of international students' difficulties in learning and give them individual help.
6. The teacher should give students study guides, distribute and announce reading assignments ahead of time so that students can have sufficient time to familiarize themselves with the materials before class.
7. More lecture, less discussion.
8. The teacher should vary the pace of the lesson and break up content into accessible units.
9. The teacher can teach international students appropriate learning strategies.
10. The teacher should use true and easy examples to help students understand a lecture.
11. The teacher should regularly get feedback from international students.
12. The teacher can slow down a little bit when teaching to make it easier for ESL students.

In total, 20 suggestions were raised for American teachers. Arts students offered more suggestions than science students. This was probably because arts students have more challenges than science students in understanding English academic lectures. A majority of the participants expected American professors to adjust their teaching methods in order to make their lectures more accessible to CESL students and other ESL students. For example, they should write key or major points on the blackboard while lecturing. Most suggestions for American professors required them to be aware of the ESL students in their classes and try to help them learn more effectively or efficiently.

CONCLUSION

Summary of Findings

The chapter investigates the effects of American classroom instructional factors on CESL students' lecture understanding at an American university. Six instructional factors are identified. First, similar to what Lebauer claimed (1984), like many ESL students who are not aware of American lecture organization, CESL students experience challenges in comprehending academic lecture. Over 60% of them reported that American professors' lecture organization influenced their academic lecture comprehension. Some commented that American professors did not organize lectures in a way that met their expectations. Second, as Upton (1989) argued, American professors often use informal and less textbook-focused teaching methodology in the classroom. More than half of the participants reported that American professors did not closely follow the textbook while lecturing. American professors' failure to follow textbooks creates challenges for them in comprehending academic lectures. Third, CESL students reported that American teachers did not write much on the board while lecturing. They are used to detailed lectures with key points written on the board (Upton, 1989). Therefore, three-fourths of them reported that American teachers' writing on the board affected their lecture comprehension. Fourth, more than 65% of the participants reported that American teachers did not usually summarize a lecture at the end of it. As Diamond, Sharp and Ory (1983) suggest, lecture summary is an essential component of an academic lecture. It was not surprising that 80% of the participants reported that lecture summaries did affect their lecture comprehension. Finally, CESL students reported that there was usually much student participation and group work in the classrooms. This is perhaps because Socratic-oriented American professors value questioning, discussing, and group work (Tweed and Lehman, 2002). As reported by CESL students, student participation and group work affected their understanding of English academic lectures.

The results of the six items show significant differences by both major and level of study. American professors' teaching methods seem to have created problems for both arts students and undergraduate students in comprehending English academic lectures. This is probably because undergraduate students are less exposed to formal academic environments and so are less familiar with American teaching methods. Some arts students comment that they experience many challenges caused by the cultural and historical differences, because they mainly learn about politics, culture, history, philosophy, languages, religion, and literature. But science students learn about universal things in the world. As quite a few participants who majored in mathematics and chemistry commented that they have little difficulty in understanding a lecture no matter what methodology the professor uses, because they recognize all the mathematical or chemical formulas and so they know what the teacher is trying to teach in class. Interestingly, the results of the six items do not show any difference by gender and length of time studying in America.

Educational Implications

Two groups of people could be the audiences of this study: CESL students and American professors. The findings in this study could be generalized for those populations. Although this study was conducted only with CESL students at an American university, the results may be applied to CESL students in other American universities and those who are still in China and want to study at American universities. Considering learning within a cultural context (Tweed and Lehman, 2002), all CESL students share common Confucian orientations. They may experience similar challenges in understanding English academic lectures. Similarly, American professors share common Socratic orientations. They need to have the same awareness of Confucian-oriented students in their classrooms.

Limitations and Directions for Future Research

The results of this study[1] were based on students' self-report data, which might not represent the real situations. This is because there are some problems with validity and reliability of self-report questionnaires. For example, the subjects might have not told the truth when they responded to the questionnaire. It is also possible that they might have not become aware of their academic challenges. What is more, this study had just 78 participants and was conducted only at one American university, which might affect the generalizibility of the study and limit the researcher's interpretation.

It is suggested that this study be replicated at another American school where there are CESL students to validate findings from this study. A slight variation might include interviewing some American professors who have CESL students in their classes. It is also suggested that a larger sample size be used to improve the chances of obtaining statistically significant differences in the analyses. Finally, this study has taken a step in defining the challenges for CESL students in understanding academic lectures at an American university. The results can be applied with caution to other non-native speakers of English or to American teachers who have international students in their classes.

REFERENCES

Algier W. (Eds.), *Improving reading and study skills*. San Francisco: Jossey-Bass.

Benson, M. J. (1989). The academic listening task: A case study. *TESOL Quarterly, 23*, 421-445.

Brown, B. (1998). Language, lectures, and learning: A language-based approach to increasing understanding. *Education, 118*, 384-393.

Brown, H. D. (1994). *Teaching by principles*. New Jersey: Prentice Hall Agents.

Brown, G., and Yule, G. (1983). *Teaching the spoken language*. Cambridge: Cambridge University Press.

Chaudron, C., and Richards, J. C. (1986). The effect of discourse markers on the comprehension of lectures. *Applied Linguistics, 7,* 113-127.

---

[1] This article was originally published in *College Student Journal.*

Chen, C. P. (1999). Common stressors among international college students: Research and counseling implications. *Journal of College Counseling, 2,* 49-65.

Chen, T. H. (1985). *Cultural differences in classrooms: A comparison of Chinese and US schooling.* Unpublished manuscript.

Conaway, M. (1982). Listening: Learning too and retention agent. In A. S. Algier and K.

Cook, J. R. S. (1975). *A communicative approach to the analysis of extended monologue discourse and its relevance to the development of teaching materials for ESP.* M. Litt. Thesis. University of Edinburgh, Scotland.

Diamond, N. A., Sharp, G. and Ory, J. C. (1983). *Improving your lecturing.* Office of Instructional and Management Services, University of Illinois at Urbana-Champaign.

Ferris D., and Tagg, T. (1996). Academic listening/speaking tasks for ESL students: Problems, suggestions, and implications. *TESOL Quarterly, 30,* 297-317.

Feng, J. H. (1991). The adaptation of students from the People's Republic of China to an American academic culture. *Reports (ERIC Document Reproduction Service No. ED 329 833).*

Flowerdew, J. (1995). Research of relevance to second language lecture comprehension: An overview. In J. Flowerdew (Ed.), *Academic listening: Research perspectives* (pp. 7-29). Cambridge: Cambridge University Press.

Flowerdew, J., and Miller, L. (1997). The teaching of academic listening and the question of authenticity. *English for Special Purposes 16,* 27-46.

Fu, D. L. (1991). A process classroom through the eyes of an outsider. *Language Arts, 68,* 121-123.

Huang, J. (2004). Voices from Chinese students: Professors' use of English affects academic listening. *College Student Journal, 38*(2), 212-223.

Institute of International Education. (2001, May 16). *98/99 opendoors on the Web.*[Selections from the book], New York. Retrieved June 15, 2001 from the World Wide Web: *http://www.opendoorsweb.org/Lead%20Stories/international_studs.htm*

Lebauer, R. S. (1984). Using lecture transcripts in EAP lecture comprehension courses. *TESOL Quarterly, 18,* 41-54.

Ma, Y., and Huang, J. (1992). *A practical guide to English teaching methodology.* Changsha: Hunan Normal University Press.

Powers, D. (1985). *A survey of academic demands related to listening skills.* (TOEFL Research Report No. 20). Princeton, NJ: Educational Testing Service.

Richards, J. (1994). *The language teaching matrix.* New York: Cambridge University Press.

Richards, J. (1983). Listening comprehension: Approach, design, procedure. *TESOL Quarterly, 17,* 219-239.

Sun, W., and Chen, G. M. (1997). *Dimensions of difficulties Mainland Chinese students encounter in the United States.* Paper presented at the 6th International Conference in Cross-Cultural Communication, Tempe, AZ. (ERIC Document Reproduction Service No. ED 408 635)

Tweed R. G., and Lehman, D. R. (2002). Learning considered within a cultural context. *American Psychologist, 57*(2), 89-99.

Upton, T. A. (1989). Chinese students, American universities, and cultural confrontation. *MinneTESOL Journal, 7,* 9-28.

Zhong, M. (1996). *Chinese students and scholars in the US: An intercultural adaptation process.* Paper presented at the 82nd Annual Meeting of the Speech Communication Association, San Diego, CA. (ERIC Document Reproduction Service No. ED 406 704)

APPENDIX

Questionnaire to Chinese ESL Students

Instructions:
1. Please read each item carefully before you choose your answer.
2. For Part I and Part III, you can answer either in English or Chinese.
3. For items that refer to teachers, lectures, and classes, please don't focus on any particular American teacher, lecture, or class. Rather, think about your American teachers, lectures, and classes in general.

I. Personal Information
Gender:
Major:
Degree sought:
Starting date of 1st semester in US:
TOEFL score:

II. Academic Listening Challenges (Related Questions Only)

14 In general, my teachers' organization of a lecture affects my comprehension.
Strongly disagree   1   2   3   4   5   Strongly agree
Any comments? _____

15. A) Do your American teachers closely follow the textbook while lecturing?
Always   1   2   3   4   5   Never
     B) How much does it affect your comprehension of the lecture?
Not at all   1   2   3   4   5   Very much
Any comments? _____

16. A) Do your teachers write a lot on the board while lecturing?
     A lot   1   2   3   4   5   Not at all
     B) How much does your teachers' writing on the board affect your lecture comprehension?
Not at all   1   2   3   4   5   Very much
Any comments? _____

17. A) How frequently do your teachers give you a lecture summary at the end of the lecture?
     Always   1   2   3   4   5   Never

   B) How much do your teachers' lecture summaries affect your lecture comprehension?
Not at all   1   2   3   4   5   Very much
Any comments? _____

20. A) Is there a lot of student participation in your class?
Always   1   2   3   4   5   Never
   B) How much does student participation affect your comprehension of the lecture?
Not at all   1   2   3   4   5   Very much
Any comments? _____

22. A) Is there a lot of group work or discussion in your class?
Always   1   2   3   4   5   Never
   B) How much does it affect your comprehension of the lecture?
Not at all   1   2   3   4   5   Very much
Any comments? _____

III. Open-Ended Question

Please give some suggestions for both the American professors and Chinese students on how to find a solution to the academic listening problems often experienced by Chinese students.

In: East Meets West
Editor: Jinyan Huang

ISBN: 978-1-62618-195-3
© 2013 Nova Science Publishers, Inc.

Chapter 11

THE FACTORS IMPACTING NORTH AMERCIAN PROFESSORS' EVALUATION OF CHINESE ESL STUDENTS' ACADEMIC WRITING

Jinyan Huang and *Chandra Foote*

Niagara University, Lewiston, New York, US

ABSTRACT

This chapter reports a study that examined score variations and differences in the reliability of ratings between Chinese ESL (CESL) - and Native English (NE-) authored papers in a graduate course at an American university. Generalizability (G-) theory was used as a framework for analysis because it is powerful in detecting rater variability and the relative contributions of multiple sources of error. The results indicate that CESL papers received consistently lower scores than NE papers. The G-coefficients for CESL and NE papers were considerably different revealing concern about the reliability of ratings of CESL papers. The significant increase in the number of CESL students pursuing graduate degrees in North American institutions warrants further research to determine the extent to which consistency differences affect the validity of the assessment of CESL students' writing and to identify ways to alleviate these differences.

INTRODUCTION

During the past two decades, there has been significant growth in the number of Chinese ESL (CESL) students pursuing graduate studies at North American universities (Canadian Bureau for International Education, 2002; Institute of International Education, 2001). Research with CESL graduate students has shown that they have difficulties in meeting graduate course expectations due to their cultural and linguistic differences (Burke and Wyatt-Smith, 1996; Huang, 2005; Huang and Klinger, 2006; Huang and Rinaldo, 2009; Jenkins, Jordan, and Weiland, 1993). These cultural and linguistic barriers prevent them from

---

* Correspondence concerning this chapter should be addressed to Dr. Jinyan Huang at *jhuang@niagara.edu*.

communicating properly with professors and meeting expectations that are commonly understood within North American higher education institutions (Jenkins, 2000; Trice, 2001).

Current research indicates that the communication gap between ESL graduate students and their professors is exacerbated in their written course work (Casanave and Hubbard, 1992). As an example, a common graduate expectation is the production of substantive course papers including literature reviews, critiques, and position papers (Wiggins, 1993). Due to their different educational systems and cultural environments, ESL graduate students struggle with these expectations. Many factors affect ESL students' writing, including their English proficiency, mother tongue, home culture, and style of written communication (Hinkel, 2003; Yang, 2001). In rating ESL students' writing, raters may differentially consider these factors. Further, empirical studies have found differences in rater behavior for ESL writing assessments (Bachman, 2000; Huang, 2008; Roberts and Cimasko, 2008). A number of studies indicate rating and rater as factors affecting the assessment of ESL writing. For example, rating methods, rating criteria, rater background, mother tongue, previous experience, and tolerance for errors have been found to influence the assessment of ESL writing (Santos, 1988; Weigle, 1999). The impact of these factors leads to questions about the consistency, precision and ultimately, the fairness of the assessment of ESL writing (Huang, 2008). This study explores the multiple factors impacting CESL student writing using generalizability (G-) theory rather than classical test theory (CTT) and attempts to extend the knowledge base by examining native English (NE) and CESL writing samples at the graduate level.

LITERATURE REVIEW

Research in second language performance assessments shows that many factors affect the rating consistency of ESL writing (Huang, 2009; Janopoulos, 1992; Santos, 1988; Roberts and Cimasko, 2008; Russikoff, 1995; Song and Caruso, 1996; Sweedler-Brown, 1993; Vann, Meyer, and Lorenz, 1984; Vann, Lorenz, and Meyer, 1991; Weigle, 1994, 1998; Weigle, Boldt, and Valsecchi, 2003). First, evaluation methods used by the raters affect their ratings of ESL writing. For example, Song and Caruso (1996) examined how evaluation methods (holistic versus analytical rating) affect English and ESL faculty's ratings of two ESL and two NE compositions at an American university. The results showed that holistic rating produced a significant difference ($p < .05$) between the English faculty and the ESL faculty, with the English faculty assigning higher scores to all four essays. However, the English faculty seemed to give more weight to the overall content and quality of the rhetorical features in rating the compositions than they did to language use when they used the analytic rating method. Russikoff (1995) also found that when the raters rated ESL compositions holistically, they paid attention only to "language use" despite the strong "content" and "organization" of these compositions.

Second, the rating criteria are a major concern in terms of the rating consistency of ESL writing. For example, professors from different disciplines tended to use different criteria for assessing different types of ESL compositions. Weigle et al (2003) found that ESL and English professors chose grammar more frequently as the most important reason for failing essays on general topics in contrast to essays that were based on reading passages and lecture notes, suggesting that ESL students may be "penalized" for poor linguistic control in essays on general topics, which are typically used in large-scale assessment writing tasks. In contrast, psychology professors chose content as the most important aspect of writing for both essays on general topics and essays that were based on reading passages and lectures notes. Similarly, Sweedler-Brown (1993) found that raters with no ESL training placed far more emphasis on the essays' linguistic features (sentence-level errors) than on the essays' strong rhetorical features.

Third, raters' professional backgrounds can have important impacts on the rating consistency of ESL compositions (Brown, 1991; Cumming, 1990; Janopoulos, 1992; Roberts and Cimasko, 2008; Song and Caruso, 1996). Raters' teaching and assessment experiences, for example, influence their rating of ESL compositions. Song and Caruso (1996) found that raters with more years of experience in teaching tended to be more lenient than raters with fewer years of teaching experience when they used holistic scoring. Cumming (1990) found that the novice raters consistently rated content and rhetorical organization higher than the expert raters. Further, their ratings for language use were significantly different from their ratings of content and rhetorical organization. However, the expert raters did not show any significant differences among their ratings of the three aspects of the compositions.

Finally, raters' tolerance for errors impacts their rating consistency of ESL compositions (Huang, 2009; Janopoulos, 1992; Santos, 1988; Vann et al., 1984; Vann et al., 1991). Research indicates that professors considered such errors as word order, verb form, and relative clause to be among the most serious and placed such errors as incorrect article and preposition usage at the "high end of the spectrum of tolerance" (Janopoulos, 1992, p. 116). Further, among faculty members in social sciences, education, humanities, biological and agricultural sciences, physical and mathematical sciences, and engineering, those from the social sciences were the most tolerant of the ESL writing errors in general (Janopoulos, 1992; Santos, 1988; Vann et al., 1984; Vann et al., 1991). These studies suggest that a "double standard" may exist in terms of faculty tolerance of ESL writing errors, with some faculty apparently willing to make allowances for the efforts of ESL writers (Janopoulos, 1992).

Most empirical studies examined the rating consistency and variability issues of ESL writing by undergraduate students. Very few studies, however, examined these issues in graduate school context. This study was intended to examine the rating consistency and variability of ESL writing by graduate students.

There are three main approaches to the detection of rating variability in performance assessment such as writing. They are: (a) the *CTT* approach; (b) the *G*-theory approach; and (c) the multi-facet Rasch approach. Research in second language performance assessments have benefited from these approaches (Huang, 2008; Lee, 2006; Lee, Kantor, and Mollaun, 2002; Sawaki, 2007). Although the multi-facet Rasch approach is also a viable alternative it was not considered within the scope of this study and has traditionally been used in more large-scale testing situations.

Although *CTT* and *G*-theory (Cronbach, Gleser, Nanda, and Rajaratnam, 1972) both have shortcomings (Eason, 1989; Lynch and McNamara, 1998), *G*-theory is more powerful than *CTT* for the detection of rater variability (Shavelson, Baxter, and Gao, 1993). *G*-theory extends the framework of *CTT* in order to take into account the multiple sources of variability that can have an effect on test scores. While *CTT* provides a single estimate of error, *G*-theory can be used to examine the relative contribution of multiple sources of error as well as their interactions on the generalizability of the assessment results (Shavelson and Webb, 1991).

Through *generalizability* (*G*-) and *decision* (*D*-) studies, researchers can evaluate the relative importance of various sources of measurement error and interpret score reliability from both norm- and criterion-referenced perspectives. Thus *G*-theory provides a comprehensive conceptual framework and methodology for analyzing more than one measurement facet (factor) simultaneously in investigations of assessment error and score dependability (Brennan, 2001).

G-theory has been increasingly used in a variety of educational performance assessment research contexts, including research in the area of second language performance assessment (Alharby, 2006; Brennan, Gao, and Colton, 1995; Brown, 2007; Brown and Bailey, 1984; Huang, 2008; Lee et al., 2002; Lee and Kantor, 2005, 2007; MacMillan, 2000; Park, 2007; Schoonen, 2005; Shavelson et al.,1993; Sudweeks, Reeve, and Bradshaw, 2005; Yamanaka, 2005). The following section reviews five empirical studies as examples of the use of *G*-theory in educational performance assessment research contexts, including the assessment of second language writing.

As early as 1993, using the California Assessment Program (CAP) science performance assessment data, Shavelson et al. (1993) conducted person-by-task-by-rater ($p \times t \times r$) random effects *G*-theory analyses. In the CAP performance assessment, the students were posed five independent tasks. A predetermined scoring rubric developed by teams of teachers in California was used to evaluate the quality of students' written responses to each of the tasks. All students' tasks were scored holistically by three raters on a 4-point scale. The results showed that the variance components associated with $p \times t$, p, and the residual were the three largest variances. However, the variance components for r, $p \times r$, $t \times r$ were close to zero. Thus the rater facet did not appear to contribute much to the variability in observed scores. By contrast, the task facet contributed substantially more to score variability. As commented by Brennan (2000), the CAP assessment results are typical of applications of *G*-theory for many programs involving performance assessments.

Two years later, Brennan et al. (1995) employed univariate and multivariate *G*-theory to examine psychometric characteristics of listening and writing tests developed by American College Testing (ACT) for its Work Keys program. For both of these tests, the same tape-recorded messages provided the stimuli for written responses that were evaluated by raters. The results of the univariate analysis using the $p \times t \times r$ design were very similar to what Shavelson et al. (1993) had found. Of particular concern were the number of messages and raters needed for adequate measurement precision. The occurrence of a relatively large person-by-message interaction suggested that at least six messages were probably required to obtain an acceptable level of reliability. Also, the analyses suggested that it was highly desirable to use at least two raters.

The results of several multivariate generalizability analyses suggested that it did not matter too much whether the same or different tasks were used for listening and writing. However, it did appear that the reliability of difference scores with relatively small numbers of tasks and raters was lower than what an investigator might like. Therefore, the multivariate results were less encouraging.

MacMillan (2000) compared three approaches (*CTT*, *G*-theory, and multi-facet Rasch) on their relative abilities to address the problem of rater variability that exists in large-scale provincial writing examinations. All three procedures identified rater variation as a problem. However, the number of raters that were identified as different varied greatly between *CTT* and the multi-facet Rasch approaches; the multi-facet Rasch analysis identified far more raters as different than the *CTT* analysis did. In contrast, the *G*-theory rater variance component and the Rasch histograms suggested little rater variation. Further, as reported by MacMillan (2000), there was a 90% agreement between *CTT* and multi-facet Rasch identification of the 10 most extreme raters but only a 50 to 60% agreement when consistency was compared.

Recently, Lee et al. (2002) examined the score dependability of writing and speaking assessment on the new TOEFL (Test of English as a Foreign Language) from the univariate and multivariate (for speaking only) *G*-theory perspectives and presented the findings from three separate *G*-theory studies. The results of these *G*-theory studies revealed that the greatest source of variation in examinees' test performances was due to differences among test takers' communication skills as measured by the writing and speaking tasks. The next greatest proportion of test variance was attributable to the interactions of person-by-task and person-by-task-by-rater. The variance due to tasks was minimal (particularly for speaking). Finally, the variance due to ratings (or raters) was close to zero, and the examinee-by-rating (rater) interaction was also very small for both writing and speaking. These results indicate that, to maximize score reliability for both speaking and writing, it would be more cost-efficient to increase the number of tasks rather than number of ratings per task.

More recently, Schoonen (2005) conducted a study in order to investigate the effects of raters and writing tasks on the generalizability of writing scores and how these effects may depend on the scoring category (content and organization versus language use), and scoring method (holistic versus analytical).

Eighty-nine grade 6 students wrote four essays, each of which was scored by five raters using two scoring methods for two categories. Further, Schoonen attempted to demonstrate the application of structural equation modeling (SEM) to estimate variance components within the context of a generalizability study.

SEM has been shown to be a flexible way to estimate variance components for different kinds of designs (Marcoulides, 1996). The results showed that the writing scores were substantially affected by facets of the writing assessment other than the writer's writing proficiency. The effects due to task and rater within task exerted a large influence on the score variance. However, these effects were in themselves dependent on the scoring categories and methods.

In summary, *G*-theory provides a very powerful theoretical framework for various performance assessment research contexts; and it has been increasingly used in second language writing assessments. Therefore, it was used as the framework for the present research.

RESEARCH QUESTIONS

Using G-theory as a framework for analysis, the purpose of this study was to assess if cultural or language factors interfere with the assessment of CESL graduate students' writing at an American university. Specifically, the following three research questions guided the study:

1. Are there significant differences in ratings of versions of the same paper wherein 1 paper has been translated to Chinese and then back to English while the other remained untranslated?
2. What are sources of score variation contributing relatively more to the score variability of the scores assigned to CESL papers in contrast to NE papers?
3. Does the reliability (e.g., generalizability coefficients for norm-referenced score interpretations) of the scores assigned to CESL papers differ from the reliability of the scores assigned to NE papers?

METHODS

The Selection of Writing Samples

The selection of the writing samples was undertaken in two phases. In Phase One, a professor within the College of Education at an American university was first invited to participate in this study. The professor then selected three position papers on a specific, assigned topic in educational assessment (see Appendix A) written by his graduate students in one class. These three papers were written by English-speaking students in his class (herein after referred to as NE papers) and evaluated by him as representing three levels of quality (high, medium, and low). Phase Two involved the selection of four CESL graduate students who majored in education and are from mainland China. One CESL graduate student translated the three papers into Chinese. Then the other three CESL graduate students translated these papers back into English, with the intention of changing the linguistic structure of the papers without affecting the overall conceptual quality (herein after referred to as CESL papers). This resulted in three separate samples of papers (student papers, p) each having two linguistic backgrounds (language, l).

The Selection of Raters

All full-time education professors at an American university were invited to rate both sets of papers. Twenty professors participated in the study. The rater-participants included 9 males and 11 females. Fourteen of the rates have completed doctoral level degrees in education. Two were doctoral candidates, and 4 were retired veteran educators with masters' degrees and at least 5 years of educational administration experience. Teaching experience in higher education ranged from 2 years to more than 25 years. Nineteen raters were native English speakers and 4 raters had completed at least 1 course in ESL teaching.

The Rating Procedure

Twenty professors marked these papers; however in order to prevent paper familiarity, each set of papers was dispersed in ten minutes intervals. Professors were provided with the rating rubric (see Appendix B) and they were required to study the rating rubric prior to marking these papers. They marked the papers holistically on a 1-6 point scale with half points allowed. There were five criteria used to evaluate each paper and these criteria were considered along with an overall assessment of quality. The criteria included: a) clear and concise statement of position, b) clear definition of meanings and terms, c) convincing evidence to support the writer's position, d) good organization and development of ideas, and e) clear, free of jargon, misspellings or grammatical errors. The levels of quality included unacceptable, inadequate, adequate, proficient, and superior.

Data Analyses

Descriptive analysis (the mean and standard deviation) and paired samples t-tests[1] for the writing scores assigned by the twenty professors were conducted for CESL and NE papers, respectively. The purpose of conducting these analyses was to examine if there was a significant mean score difference between CESL and NE papers.

Within *G*-theory framework, data were further analyzed in the following three stages: a) paper-by-rater-by-language random effects *G*-study; b) paper-by-rater random effects *G*-studies, and c) calculation of *G*-coefficients.

Paper-by-rater-by-language random effects G-study. A paper-by-rater-by-language (*p x r x l*) random effects *G*-study analysis was conducted. The purpose of this *G*-study was to obtain variance component estimates for the seven independent sources of variation: paper (*p*), rater (*r*), language (*l*), paper-by-rater (*p x r*), paper-by-language (*p x l*), language-by-rater (*l x r*), and paper-by-rater-by-language (*p x r x l*).

Paper-by-rater random effects G-studies. Two separate paper-by-rater (*p x r*) random effects *G*-studies were conducted for CESL papers and for NE papers.

The main purpose of these *G*-studies was to obtain information for comparison between CESL and NE students in terms of score variability and reliability. It was expected that some differences would be found between CESL and NE students. With the implementation of these *G*-studies, the three independent sources of variation, namely, paper (*p*), rating (*r*), and paper-by-rater (*p x r*) for each language group were obtained. Using the obtained variance components, *G*-coefficients for each language group were then calculated for examining the reliability.

Calculation of G-coefficients: The following formula was used for the calculation of *G*-coefficient ($E\rho^2$), which is the reliability for norm-referenced score interpretations (Brennan, 2001):

$$E\rho^2 = \frac{\sigma_s^2}{\sigma_s^2 + \sigma_\delta^2} = \frac{\sigma_s^2}{\sigma_s^2 + \dfrac{\sigma_{sr}^2}{n_r}}$$

(1)

where σ_s^2 is the universe score variance, σ_δ^2 is the relative error variance.

---

[1] Each set of paper has two versions (English and Chinese) and the two versions are considered as one paper because they are the same conceptually.

Based on the paper-by-rater ($p \times r$) random effects G-studies results, G-coefficients for each language group (CESL versus NE) were calculated. The purpose of calculating the G-coefficients was to answer the third research question: Does reliability of the scores assigned to CESL papers differ from the reliability of the scores assigned to NE papers? The computer program GENOVA (Crick and Brennan, 1983) was used for the G-studies. GENOVA is a computer program used to estimate the variance components for the main and interaction effects and their standard errors where the design is balanced. The program also computes the G-coefficients ($E\rho^2$) and dependability coefficients ($\Phi(\lambda)$) for different values of the cut-score λ.

RESULTS

Descriptive Results

Table 11.1 provides the descriptive statistics for the CESL and NE paper data used in the analyses. As mentioned above, each paper was rated holistically by twenty independent raters on a 6-point scale. Table 11.1 provides both the mean and standard deviation of the ratings of each paper assigned by twenty raters. Comparing the results of the CESL and NE students, the results show that all three CESL papers had consistently lower ratings than the corresponding NE papers. Further, as shown in Table 11.2, paired samples t-tests results show that CESL papers #1 and 3 had significantly lower ratings than NE papers # 1 and 3 ($p < .01$). The ratings for the second paper were not significantly different across languages.

Table 11.1. Descriptive Statistics

Paper	CESL		NE	
	Mean	SD	Mean	SD
1	3.43	.91	4.73	.95
2	3.25	1.07	3.35	1.32
3	3.83	1.44	4.98	.91

* *Note*: N (rater) = 20.

Table 11.2. Paired Samples t-Tests Results

	Paired Differences			t	df	Sig. (2-tailed)
	Mean	Std. Deviation	Std. Error Mean			
Pair 1: CESL-EN (Paper #1)	1.3000	1.2183	.2724	4.772	19	.000 *
Pair 2: CESL-EN (Paper #2)	.1000	1.3436	.3004	.333	19	.743
Pair 3: CESL-EN (Paper #3)	1.1500	1.2784	.2859	4.023	19	.001 *

* *Note*: indicates significant difference at the .01 significance level.

Paper-by-Rater-by-Language Random Effects G-Study Results

The results presented in Table 11.3 show that the residual yielded the largest variance component (33.47% of the total variance). The residual contains the variability due to the interaction between raters, languages, papers, and other unexplained systematic and unsystematic sources of error. Rater (r) yielded the second largest variance component (19.05% of the total variance), indicating that raters differed greatly from one another in terms of leniency of marking these papers. Language (l) yielded the third largest variance component (14.62% of the total variance), suggesting that there was a large difference in the writing scores that could be attributed to language group. Paper (p), the object of measurement, yielded the fourth largest variance component (10.89% of the total variance), suggesting that the three selected papers are different in terms of quality. Paper-by-language (pl) yielded the fifth largest variance component (9.45% of the total variance), indicating that papers are relatively different in terms of qualities across languages. Language-by-rater (lr) yielded the sixth largest variance component (9.22% of the total variance), suggesting that there was inconsistency in terms of rating severity or leniency across languages.

**Table 11.3. Variance Components for a Random Effects
p x l x r G-Study Design**

Source of Variability	df	σ^2	%
p	2	0.2093	10.89
l	1	0.2811	14.62
r	19	0.3662	19.05
pl	2	0.1816	9.45
pr	38	0.0636	3.31
lr	19	0.1772	9.22
plr	39	0.6434	33.47
Total	119	1.9225	100

The percentage of the paper-by-rater (pr) variance component was relatively small (3.31% of the total variance), indicating that raters did not mark all papers very differently.

Paper-by-Rater Random Effects G-Studies Results

The paper-by-rater random effects *G*-studies results for both CESL and NE papers are presented in Table 11.4. The results for the CESL papers show that rater (r) yielded the largest variance component (52.05% of the total variance), suggesting that raters differed extremely from one another in terms of leniency of marking the CESL papers. The residual yielded the second largest variance component (43.95% of the total variance). The residual contains the variability due to the interaction between raters and papers, and other unexplained systematic and unsystematic sources of error. However, the percentage for the object of measurement (papers) was very small (4.01% of the total variance), suggesting that the CESL papers are relatively the same in terms of quality.

The results for the NE papers show that the residual yielded the second largest variance component (42.43% of the total variance). The object of measurement, paper (p), yielded the second largest variance component (38.52% of the total variance), suggesting that the three selected NE papers are very different in terms of quality. Rater (r) yielded the third variance component (19.05% of the total variance), suggesting that raters differed considerably from one another in terms of leniency of marking the three NE papers.

Table 11.4. Variance Components for Random Effects
p x r G-Study Designs

Language Group	Source of Variability	df	σ^2	%
CESL	p	2	0.0561	4.01
	r	19	0.7279	52.04
	pr	38	0.6147	43.95
	Total	59	1.3987	100
EN	p	2	0.7257	38.52
	r	19	0.359	19.05
	pr	38	0.7993	42.43
	Total	59	1.884	100

In summary, the results of the paper-by-rater-by-language random effects G-study and the paper-by-rater random effects G-studies indicate that the great source of score variation for the original NE papers was due to differences among students' English writing skills as measured by the position paper. This suggests that, as intended, the position paper did distinguish among NE students.

However, the greatest source of score variation for the CESL versions was due to differences among raters, not differences among students' English writing skills as measured by the position paper. The large variance due to language group (l) shows that there was a large score difference between the original NE papers and the corresponding CESL papers. The variance due to rater for CESL papers was over twice as much as the rater variance for NE papers. These differences may due to either the quality difference between the original NE papers and the CESL papers or rating bias against CESL writing samples.

Calculation of G-Coefficients

Using formula 1 and the paper-by-rater random effects G-studies variance component results, the G-coefficients for each language group were calculated. The results are presented in Table 11.5. As shown, the G-coefficient obtained for CESL papers for the current twenty-rater scenario was .65; however, the G-coefficient for the original NE papers was .95.

Table 11.5. Summary of G-coefficients

Number of Papers	Number of Raters	G-Coefficients CESL	EN
3	1	.08	.48
3	2	.15	.64
3	3	.22	.73
3	4	.27	.78
3	5	.31	.82
3	6	.35	.84
3	7	.39	.86
3	8	.42	.88
3	9	.45	.89
3	10	.48	.90
3	11	.50	.91
3	12	.52	.91
3	13	.54	.92
3	14	.56	.93
3	15	.58	.93
3	16	.59	.94
3	17	.61	.94
3	18	.62	.94
3	19	.63	.95
3	20	.65	.95

DISCUSSION AND CONCLUSION

The first research question attempted to determine if there would be significant differences between two versions of the same paper when one had undergone language translation from English to Chinese and back to English while the other remained in its original format. In all three instances, the NE version had mean ratings higher than the CESL version and for two of the three papers (i.e., Papers # 1 and 3) there was a significant difference in these ratings. This indicates that although the two versions of these papers had the same conceptual quality, they were assessed differently based on their linguistic structure.

The second research question examined the differences in score variation between CESL and NE papers. The results showed that differences in score variation did exist between CESL and NE papers. First, there was a large effect for both language and language-by-paper and language-by-rater interactions, which are unwanted variations. As previously discussed, these findings suggest that there was a large difference between the writing scores received by the CESL and NE papers. Together with the descriptive results and the large variance component for language, the CESL papers received consistently lower scores than the NE papers. Second, the desired variance associated with the object of measurement (i.e., papers) was much smaller for CESL papers (4.01% of the total variance) than for NE papers (38.5% of the total variance). These differences suggest poorer reliability in the ratings of the CESL papers. The third research question focused on the differences in the reliability of the scores received by the CESL and NE papers. As mentioned above, there was a large difference in the G-coefficients for CESL and NE papers and this difference had considerable impact on the rating reliability of CESL papers. Together, the differences in terms of the desired and unwanted variations between the CESL and NE scores and the lower *G*-coefficient for CESL papers raise a potential question about the fairness of the writing scores assigned to CESL papers. If the ratings of CESL and NE papers are not equally reliable, then fairness may become a concern because there should be no large differences in the rating variability and reliability of scores assigned to CESL and NE papers (Huang, 2008; Johnson, Penny, and Gordon, 2000). The differences in accuracy and precision may be due to factors outside of the writing skills of CESL students. However, further exploration of these issues is needed to determine if the differences were due to fairness issues or actual systematic differences in English writing skills.

The present study was limited in the following three ways. First, due to the fundamental differences between English and Chinese and also the CESL students' English translation and writing skills, the use of English-Chinese translation and Chinese-English back translation might have created considerable differences between the NE papers and their corresponding Chinese versions. Second, lack of formal rater training before marking might have produced an impact on the results of this study. The twenty raters who participated in the study are very different in their professional backgrounds. Research shows that the scores that raters assign to ESL papers may fluctuate due to many factors; for example, the scoring methods used (holistic versus analytic), the differences in raters' application of scoring criteria, and the differences in raters' linguistic and professional backgrounds (Janopoulos, 1992; Roberts and Cimasko, 2008; Song and Caruso, 1996). Rater training, however, can minimize the differences caused by these factors (Weigle, 1994, 1998) and modify raters' expectations of good writing by clarifying for the raters both the task demands and writer characteristics (Huot, 1990). Further, rater training is especially effective for inexperienced raters of ESL papers to minimize the differences in ratings (Weigle, 1994). The fact that university professors evaluating graduate students' written assignments in authentic settings do not typically receive rater training provides a counter argument to this potential limitation.

Finally, only holistic scoring was employed in this study. Research shows that the use of different scoring methods (holistic vs. analytic) may affect the reliability and validity of the rating of ESL papers (Russikoff, 1995). Since raters provided only a holistic grade based on a number of criteria it may be that a single criterion focused on writing clarity, the use of jargon, misspellings, and grammatical error was the most influential factor in the overall grade. It will be interesting to see if analytical scoring can yield similar results in terms of rating variability and reliability.

In light of the limitations, the following two conclusions were reached. First, there was a consistency in the degree to which CESL papers were underscored as compared to NE papers. Further, the main effect for language was large, indicating large differences in the assigned scores between CESL and NE papers. As previously discussed, this difference may be due to the use of translation and back translation procedures used in this study. Other factors may also be related to these findings; therefore, there is a need for further exploration of this issue. Second, there is still large unexplained variability in language groups. As previously mentioned, the residual contains the variability due to the interaction between raters and papers, and other unexplained systematic and unsystematic sources of error. Residual effects can indicate hidden facets (Brennan, 2001). For example, "gender" and "occasion" were not considered in this study. The variance of the hidden facets is included in the residual variance, thus leading to a larger residual than when the facet is explicitly considered.

Overall, the study provides initial evidence that the ratings of CESL and NE papers result in differences in terms of consistency and precision. Further examination using *G*-theory and multi-facet Rasch approaches may determine the extent to which these consistency differences affect the fairness and accuracy of the assessment of CESL graduate students' English writing skills and to find ways to alleviate these differences. The findings in this study[2], taken in consideration with past research in this area, offer some insight to CESL students seeking to improve their writing and professors wishing to improve their consistency of grading. Our primary finding is that despite equity in conceptual content, differences in linguistic structure lead to greater variation in grading. The CESL student writer should therefore concentrate on clarity of conceptual presentation following accepted linguistic structure. The professor would do well to establish a clear scoring guide, holistic or analytic, that targets conceptual understanding over linguistic presentation. Adherence to such a scoring guide may also minimize the inconsistency in grading that more greatly impacts CESL writers as the present study, and many other studies have demonstrated.

APPENDICES

Appendix A

Position Paper on the Use of High-Stakes Tests to Measure Learning
Using standard English, write a coherent, unified, multi-paragraph mini-position paper of approximately 1000 words on the topic below.

Critics of high-stakes tests (i.e., tests that are used to make decisions that are of prominent educational, financial, or social impact) say that they result in teaching to the test and that this is what is responsible for test score increases rather than real learning improvement. Keeping this in mind, argue *for OR against* the use of high-stakes tests to measure learning.

Appendix B

Holistic Rating Rubric for the Position Paper

Holistic Rating Rubric (6-point scale; half point allowed)

	The FIVE criteria for rating the position paper are: 1) it has a clear and concise statement of position; 2) it contains clear definitions and meanings of terms; 3) it presents convincing evidence to support the writer's position; 4) it shows good organization and development of ideas; and 5) it is clear, free of jargon, misspellings or grammatical errors.
1	The *one* paper meets NONE of the five criteria and it is unacceptable.
2	The *two* paper meets only ONE criterion and it is unacceptable.
3	The *three* paper meets only TWO criteria and it is inadequate.
4	The *four* paper meets THREE criteria and it is adequate.
5	The *five* paper meets FOUR criteria and it is proficient.
6	The *six* paper meets all FIVE criteria and it is superior.

[2] This article was originally published in *Language Assessment Quarterly*.

REFERENCES

Alharby, E. R. (2006). A comparison between two scoring methods, holistic vs analytic, using two measurement models, the generalizability theory and many-facet Rasch measurement, within the context of performance assessment. *Unpublished PhD dissertation at The Pennsylvania State University,* State College, PA.

Bachman, L. (2000). Modern language testing at the turn of the century: Assuring that what we count counts. *Language Testing, 17*(1), 1-42.

Brennan, R. L. (2000). Performance assessments from perspective of generalizability theory. *Applied Psychological Measurement, 24*(4), 339-353.

Brennan, R. L. (2001). *Statistics for social science and public policy: Generalizability theory.* New York: Springer-Verlag.

Brennan, R. L., Gao, X., and Colton, D. A. (1995). Generalizability analyses of Work Keys listening and writing tests. *Educational and Psychological Measurement, 55,* 157-176.

Brown, J. D. (2007). Multiple views of L1 writing score reliability. *Second Language Studies* (Working papers), *25(2),* 1-31.

Brwon, J. D., and Bailey, K. M. (1984). A categorical instrument for scoring second language writing skills. *Language Learning, 34*, 21-42.

Brown, J. D. (1991). Do English and ESL faculties rate writing samples differently? *TESOL Quarterly, 25*(4), 587-603.

Burke, E., and Wyatt-Smith, C. (1996). Academic and non-academic difficulties: Perceptions of graduate non-English speaking background students [electronic database]. *TESL-EJ, 2,* Available: http://www- writing.Berkeley.edu/TESL-EJ/ej05/al.html.

Canadian Bureau for International Education. (2002). *International student numbers hit record high, but Canada offers dwindling support for African students.* Retrieved October 28, 2002 from the World Wide Web: http://www.cbie.ca/news/index_e.cfm?folder=releasesandpage=rel_2002-04-15_e.

Casanave, C. P., and Hubbard, P. (1992). The writing assignments and writing problems of doctoral students: Faculty perceptions, pedagogical issues, and needed research. *English for Specific Purposes, 11*, 33-49.

Crick, J. E., and Brennan, R. L. (1983). *GENOVA: A general purpose analysis of variance system. Version* 2.1. Iowa City, IA: American College Testing Program.

Cronbach, L. J., Gleser, G. C., Nanda, H., and Rajaratnam, N. (1972). *The dependability of behavioral measurements: Theory of generalizability for scores and profiles.* New York: Wiley.

Cumming, A. (1990). Expertise in evaluating second language composition. *Language Testing, 7*, 31-51.

Eason, S. (1989). *Why generalizability theory yields better results than classical test theory.* Paper presented at the annual meeting of the Mid-South Educational Research Association, Little Rock, AR. (ERIC Document Reproduction Service No.ED 314 434).

Hinkel, E. (2003). Simplicity without elegance: Features of sentences in L1 and L2 academic texts. *TESOL Quarterly, 37*, 275-301.

Huang, J. (2005). Challenges of academic listening in English: Reports by Chinese students. *College Student Journal, 39*(3), 553-569.

Huang, J. (2008). How accurate are ESL students' holistic writing scores on large-scale assessments? - A generalizability theory approach. *Assessing Writing, 13(3)*, 201-218.

Huang, J. (2009). Factors affecting the assessment of ESL students' writing. *International Journal of Applied Educational Studies, 5*(1).

Huang, J., and Klinger, D. (2006). Chinese graduate students at North American universities: Learning challenges and coping strategies. *The Canadian and International Education Journal, 35*(2), 48-61.

Huang, J., and Rinaldo, V. (2009). Factors affecting Chinese graduate students' cross-cultural learning at North American universities. *International Journal of Applied Educational Studies, 4(1)*, 1-13.

Huot, B. A. (1990). Reliability, validity, and holistic rating: What we know and what we need to know. *College Composition and Communication, 41*, 201–213.

Institute of International Education. (2001). *98/99 opendoors on the Web.* [Selections from the book], New York. Retrieved June 15, 2002 from the World Wide Web: http://www.opendoorsweb.org/Lead%20Stories/ international_studs.htm.

Janopoulos, M. (1992). University faculty tolerance of NS and NNS writing errors: A comparison. *Journal of Second Language Writing, 1*(2),109-121.

Jenkins, S. (2000). Cultural and linguistic miscues: A case study of international teaching assistant and academic faculty miscommunication. *International Journal of Intercultural Relations, 24*, 477-501.

Jenkins, S., Jordan, M. K., and Weiland, P. O. (1993). The role of writing in graduate engineering education: A survey of faculty beliefs and practices. *English for Specific Purposes, 12*, 51-67.

Johnson, R. L., Penny, J., and Gordon, B. (2000). The relation between score resolution methods and interrater reliability: An empirical study of an analytic rating rubric. *Applied Measurement in Education, 13*(2), 121-138.

Lee, Y. (2006). Dependability of scores for a new ESL speaking assessment consisting of integrated and independent tasks. *Language Testing, 23*(2), 131-166.

Lee, Y., and Kantor, R. (2005). *Dependability of ESL writing test scores: Evaluating prototype tasks and alternative rating schemes*. TOEFL Monograph MS-31. Princeton, NJ: ETS.

Lee, Y., and Kantor, R. (2007). Evaluating prototype tasks and alternative rating schemes for a new ESL writing test through *G*-theory. *International Journal of Testing, 7*(4), 353-385.

Lee, Y., Kantor, R., and Mollaun, P. (2002). Score dependability of the writing and speaking sections of new TOEFL. *Paper presented at the annual meeting of National Council on Measurement in education*, New Orleans, LA.

Lynch, B. K., and McNamara, T. F. (1998). Using G-theory and many-facet Rasch measurement in the development of performance assessments of the ESL speaking skills of immigrants. *Language Testing, 15*(2), 158-180.

MacMillan, P. D. (2000). Classical, generalizability, and multifaceted Rasch detection of interrater variability in large, sparse data sets. *Journal of Experimental Education, 68(2)*, 167-190.

Park, T. (2007). *Investigating the construct validity of the Community Language Program (CLP) English Writing Test*. Unpublished PhD dissertation at Teachers College, Columbia University, New York, NY.

Roberts, F., and Cimasko, T. (2008). Evaluating ESL: Making sense of university professors' responses to second language writing. *Journal of Second Language Writing, 17*, 125-143.

Russikoff, K. A. (1995). *A comparison of writing criteria: Any differences?* Paper presented at the annual meeting of the Teachers of English to Speakers of Other languages, Long Beach, CA.

Santos, T. (1988). Professors' reactions to the writing of nonnative-speaking students. *TESOL Quarterly, 22*(1), 69-90.

Sawaki, Y. (2007). Construct validation of analytic rating scales in a speaking assessment: Reporting a score profile and a composite. *Language Testing, 24*(3), 355-390.

Schoonen, R. (2005). Generalizability of writing scores: an application of structural equation modeling. *Language Testing, 22*(1), 1-30.

Shavelson, R. J., and Webb, N. M. (1991). *Generalizability theory: A primer*. Newbury Park, CA: Sage.

Shavelson, R. J., Baxter, G. P., and Gao, X. (1993). Sampling variability of performance assessments. *Journal of Educational Measurement, 30*, 215-232.

Song, B., and Caruso, I. (1996). Do English and ESL faculty differ in evaluating the essays of Native English-Speaking, and ESL students? *Journal of Second Language Writing, 5*(2), 163-182.

Sudweeks, R. R., Reeve, S., and Bradshaw, W. S. (2005). A comparison of generalizability theory and many-facet Rasch measurement in an analysis of college sophomore writing. *Assessing Writing, 9*, 239-261.

Sweedler-Brown, C. O. (1993). ESL essay evaluation: The influence of sentence-level and rhetorical features. *Journal of Second Language Writing, 2*, 3-17.

Trice, A. G. (2001). Faculty perceptions of graduate international students: The benefits and challenges. *Paper presented at the 26th Annual Meeting of the Association for the Study of Higher Education,* Richmond, VA. (ERIC Document Reproduction Service No. ED 457 816).

Vann, R., Lorenz, F., and Meyer, D. (1991). Error gravity: Faculty response to errors in the written discourse of non-native speakers of English. In L. Hamp-Lyons (Ed.), *Assessing second language writing in academic contexts* (pp. 181-195). Norwood, NJ: Ablex.

Vann, R., Meyer, D., and Lorenz, F. (1984). Error gravity: A study of faculty opinion of ESL errors. *TESOL Quarterly, 18*, 427-440.

Weigle, S. C. (1994). Effects of training on raters of ESL compositions. *Language Testing, 11*, 197-223.

Weigle, S. C. (1998). Using FACETS to model rater training effects. *Language Testing, 15*(2), 263-287.

Weigle, S. C. (1999). Investigating rater/prompt interactions in writing assessment: Quantitative and qualitative approaches. *Assessing Writing, 6*(2), 145-178.

Weigle, S. C., Boldt, H., and Valsecchi, M. I. (2003). Effects of task and rater background on the evaluation of ESL writing: A pilot study. *TESOL Quarterly, 37*(2), 345-354.

Wiggins, G. (1993). *Assessing student performance: Exploring the purpose and limits of testing*. San Francisco, CA: Jossey-Bass.

Yamanaka, H. (2005). Using generalizability theory in the evaluation of L2 writing. *JALT Journal, 27*(2), 169-185.

Yang, Y. (2001). *Chinese interference in English writing: Cultural and linguistic differences.* (ERIC Document Reproduction Service No. ED 461 992).

In: East Meets West
Editor: Jinyan Huang

ISBN: 978-1-62618-195-3
© 2013 Nova Science Publishers, Inc.

Chapter 12

NORTH AMERICAN PROFESSORS' SOCIAL SUPPORT FACILITATES CHINESE ESL STUDENTS' ACADEMIC LEARNING

*R. Michael Smith** and Ling Zhou*
Niagara University, Lewiston, New York, US

ABSTRACT

This chapter is a case study based on the first-year experiences of a two-year longitudinal study. It describes how a North American professor provided an extended social support system for a Chinese ESL (CESL) student in an effort to facilitate the student's academic learning. Focusing on Maslow's hierarchy of needs as the conceptual framework, the study describes how each of the student's needs: physiological; safety; love and belongingness; self-esteem; and self-actualization were met to facilitate the learning process and academic success of the CESL student. The results of the study will provide answers to assist university mentors who are willing to provide extended social support facilities to ESL students in an effort to improve their academic achievement and intercultural experiences.

INTRODUCTION

According to the Institute of International Education ((IIE) (2001) and the Canadian Bureau for International Education (CBIE) (2002), Chinese ESL (CESL) students from the People's Republic of China (PRC) are the largest single group of ESL students studying in North American universities, and their numbers continue to grow. In addition, approximately 80% of the students in this group are enrolled in graduate university programs throughout North America.

---

* Correspondence concerning this chapter should be addressed to Dr. R. Michael Smith at *msmith@niagara.edu*.

Despite the rising numbers, CESL graduate students are often ill-prepared for the cultural differences that they will face, and there is a great need for more inclusive mentoring programs to ensure the social well-being and academic success of all CESL students.

Some problems they encounter are related to specific needs as outlined by Maslow (McLeod, 2012; Cherry 2012), and include but are not limited to: English language proficiency, Chinese language influence, North American educational culture, Chinese educational background, study skills or strategies, financial and emotional issues (Chen, 1999; Feng, 1991; Huang, 1998; Huang, 2004, 2005, 2006; Liu, 1994; Sun and Chen, 1997; Upton, 1989; Yuan, 1982; Zhong, 1996). As a result, these factors can impede their academic learning (Huang and Klinger, 2006; Lin, 2002). However, if mentorships can be expanded to extend social support facilities to CESL students in an effort to meet the above needs, the results could translate into improved academic achievement and intercultural experiences. And, while there is a plethora of research on the benefits of mentoring and supporting foreign students in North American universities, there is little published research in the form of longitudinal studies that describe the entire mentoring process from the student's application to university to the culminating experience of graduation. Hence, the purpose of this chapter was to provide insights into the effective implementation of a more inclusive mentoring program for CESL graduate students at North American universities. The following three questions informed the chapter: a) What steps can be implemented in a mentoring program to meet each of the five needs as defined by Maslow? b) How can the professor (mentor) gain a better understanding of cultural diversity through the experience? c) What are the key factors for developing a strong mentorship between the professor and the CESL student?

CONCEPTUAL FRAMEWORK

Maslow's hierarchy of needs served as the conceptual framework for this longitudinal case study. As such, the researchers report and reflect on how a more inclusive mentoring process supported the various needs: physiology; safety; love and belongingness; self-esteem; and self-actualization in an effort to facilitate the social well-being and academic success of all CESL students.

According to Maslow (McLeod, 2012; Cherry 2012), *physiological needs* are the basic needs that are vital to survival, such as water, air, food, sleep, clothing, and shelter; *safety needs* involve security and safety from both emotional and physical harm; *love and belongingness needs* include the need for love, affection, and belonging, such as relationships with family and friends, social, community, or religious groups; *esteem needs* deal with feeling good about one's self such as self-esteem, personal worth, social recognition, and accomplishment; and *self-actualization*, the highest level, is concerned with personal growth, altruistic principles, and the fulfillment of one's potential.

SUMMARY OF PREVIOUS LITERATURE

Much has been researched about the importance of diversity at North American universities and the mentoring of international students, CESL students in particular.

According to Pritchard (2012), despite the numerous mentoring programs, the majority of university mentors still feel unprepared for the role which results in a lack of confidence in their ability to support students (Duffy, 2004). "The main challenges facing mentors are understanding the needs of each individual and adapting and developing strategies in order to support them effectively ... By recognizing the need to gain insight into the students' individual needs, mentors will be able to identify any concerns and develop action plans in order to alleviate them" (Pritchard, 2012, p. 119).

The major challenges in academic learning for CESL students as described by Huang and Klinger (2006) include a) financial difficulties; b) problems in using English for academic purposes; c) frustrations in becoming a permanent resident; d) difficulty in adapting to classroom learning environment; e) lack of critical thinking skills; f) acculturation problems; and g) loneliness and academic anxiety. These challenges can all be either directly or indirectly related to Maslow's hierarchy of needs as a starting point for uncovering the key to successfully mentoring CESL students in the North American university environment; however, it is apparent that the greater the social support system, the greater the chance for academic success and improved intercultural understanding.

METHODOLOGY

About the Two-year Longitudinal Case Study

Professor *A* and CESL Student *B* were the two participants for this study which describes an extended social support system (mentoring environment) for a CESL student in an effort to facilitate the student's academic learning and intercultural understanding. This chapter only describes the first year experiences in a two-year longitudinal case study.

In September 2007, for his sabbatical, a New York State university professor (Professor *A*) accepted a one-year position teaching English-as-a-foreign-language (EFL) at a private university in Shanghai, PRC. In Shanghai, he was introduced to a young Chinese woman (Student *B*) who served as a translator and cultural facilitator for him. During their conversations, she expressed an interest in applying to graduate school in the United States, and because he was impressed with her English-speaking ability, her social skills, and outgoing personality, he offered to assist her with the graduate school search and application process.

At the completion of his sabbatical, Professor *A* returned to New York State in August of 2008 and remained in contact with Student *B*. In 2011, Professor *A* returned to China for a brief visit during the first two weeks of January. He met with Student *B* and when she expressed a sincere interest in applying to the MBA program at his university, he offered to assist her with the application and provide free room and board at his home which was conveniently located within a mile of the university campus.

In June 2011, Student *B* applied to the university and forwarded her undergraduate transcripts and completed application forms to the school. According to the student, the staff at the university admissions' office was extremely helpful in organizing her documents, and her visa application was accepted at her immigration interview in China. As a result, she booked her flight to the US and arrived in New York State on September 6, 2011.

Data Collection and Analysis

The data for this study were collected during two, three-hour interviews with Professor *A* and Student *B*. The interviews were transcribed and analyzed according to the research questions. Specifically, the following three questions informed the chapter: a) What steps were taken in this mentoring program in order to meet each of Student *B*'s five needs as defined by Maslow? b) How can Professor *A* (mentor) gain a better understanding of cultural diversity through the experience? c) What are the key factors for developing a strong mentorship between mentoring professors and the CESL students?

RESULTS

During the course of the two interviews, the five needs: physiological, safety, love and belongingness, self-esteem, and self-actualization were discussed in this section.

Physiological Needs

Student *B* believes that her physiological needs are more than adequately met. When she arrived at her new residence in the US, she was pleased to have her own bedroom with a new queen-size bed and mattress, ceiling fan, central air conditioning, a chair and study desk accented with an arrangement of Chinese bamboo in an oriental vase and terra cotta warrior candles. Also, in the house she had unlimited access to wireless high-speed Internet, her own closet with extra linens, a large window that can be opened to access fresh air, and plenty of extra storage in the basement and attic. Her bedroom was next door to a full bathroom and she had full access to the kitchen to prepare her congee, rice, dumplings, tomato and egg, and other Chinese dishes.

According to Student *B*, Professor *A*'s house is conveniently located about a ten-minute bike ride and 30-minute walk from the campus. "I love all kinds of exercise, and don't mind the distance at all but for some other Chinese person; it would have been more convenient if the house were closer to the University. The only thing that bothered me was that Professor *A* redecorated the house two months before my arrival and turned the basement into his own living space. I was really bothered by the fact that Professor *A* was living in the basement, even though he assured me that it was absolutely fine and he enjoyed living there. I felt more comfortable after his daughter told me that he preferred living in his 'Man Cave' living quarters."

It is very important to Student *B* to be able to enjoy the comforts and familiarity of a home-cooked, authentic Chinese meal. Fortunately, after befriending the Chinese family who lived a block away, she would travel with them to a neighboring city to purchase authentic Chinese groceries and then return home to cook Chinese dumplings and other Chinese dishes. (She reported being shocked and excited that so many Chinese vegetables and snacks were available and reasonably priced within a 30-minute drive.) In addition, the three-year old son of the Chinese neighbors has the same September birth date and the family joined them for a birthday celebration in Professor *A*'s backyard.

Student *B* is also appreciative of having her own space and access to all parts of the house. This was apparent when she stated, "Living with Professor *A* and his family brings so much benefit that I would not have if I were living in the dorms. First, it is great to have my own space where I can study, and stay up late reading, watching movies, listening to the music and chatting with family and friends online. Second, it is great to being able to cook instead of eating in the school cafeteria. This makes up nearly 70% of my life in America."

Safety and Security Needs

Student *B*'s safety needs are also met in numerous ways. Regarding safety issues and physical harm, Professor *A* has four bicycles in his storage shed and during the first months that Student *B* lived at his house, they would often take rides around the area so Student *B* could feel comfortable and know the area, streets, places of interest, and the neighbors. There were also bicycle helmets in the shed; however, wearing the headgear was unfortunately not a practice that Student *B* adopted. She does, however, have a fear of dogs and expressed her gratitude that there were no pets in the house.

Student *B* is also very physically active and as she stated, "I was happy to know the athletic membership was included in the student benefits and I don't have to pay for the gym; I take full advantage of all the fitness facilities and work out almost every day, unlike most Chinese females who are not big fan of exercises. I would walk or ride my bike to the gym and when I would work out in the evening and it was dark, Professor *B* would pick me up and sometimes even let me drive the car home once I passed my beginner's driving license."

Professor *A* describes Student *B* as being very respectful of her family. "Unlike many Chinese children, she also has a sibling brother whom she converses with on a weekly basis and updates her parents regularly as to her experiences, accomplishments, and the fact that she feels very safe in the community and school setting."

Financial security is also important to Student *B*. According to her, "It is helpful to live with someone who knows the American banking system, as it is a totally different system from China. I got my debit card without a hitch with the help from Professor *A*. It allows me to be more independent and it is also a huge relief for me being able to use Professor *A*'s credit card to pay off my tuition fee because my debit card receives funds from China every few months but if anything went wrong in between, I can still pay my tuition fee by using his credit card and don't have to worry about being kicked out of school or having to pay late fee." (N.B. it is also beneficial to Professor *A*, because he receives 1% cash back on his credit card purchases and Student *B* always pays him in full with a week.)

Love and Belongingness Needs

Professor *A* states that student *B* is very personable and has an outgoing personality and great sense of humor. Her cheerful and caring attitude allows her to make friends easily, and as such, her Love and Belongingness needs have a strong foundation. Also, Professor *A* attempts to provide opportunities for her to meet a variety of new people whenever possible. His daughter also lived in the same house until the end of January and is about the same age as Student *B*. They both got along well and they did a lot of girls' talk together. According to

Student *B*, however, "it wouldn't be much different if Professor *A* had a son, because the fact is that as long as the two people are about the same age and have things in common, there will be a lot to talk about but one thing for sure is the rooms won't be as tidy as now." Professor *A* and Student *B* talked about his family members from time to time, and she said "it was great to finally meet up with them and match the names with people in person. At his family's Christmas dinner, his brother-in-law kept calling me Korean. It was the first Christmas dinner I ever had and I really appreciated that I had a chance to learn how family members here interact with each other."

Student *B* arrived on campus one day after classes officially started, leaving her no time to join in orientations and become acquainted with the campus, professors, other students, clubs and services. She stated, "Looking back now, I would like to have arrived one week earlier and attend some of the orientation in order to know the area better, the facility on campus and maybe make some friends. As a matter of fact, I did experience a little bit of a problem not knowing the campus layout. I was looking for the library and was embarrassed when I walked into the girls' dorm instead, thinking it was the library. The front desk lady was so confused when I handed her my student ID card and told her she needs to lend me a book."

Self-esteem

According to Professor *A*, "Self-esteem is often dependent on the day, the conditions, and the situation. In China, her native country, today, Student B is looked upon as extremely successful by her family, friends, and peers, especially when one considers the gender bias in the country and how much more difficult it is for a female to enjoy the same educational and financial opportunities and successes as the male population. Nevertheless, I believe that Student *B*, like most students, experiences some insecurity at times because she is not totally apprised of and comfortable with all of the American customs, slang, nuances, and cultural differences. However, her excellent grades, scholarship awards, faculty support and guidance, and the friendly advice that she receives from fellow students and the administrative staff more than offset any negative thought that may arise concerning cultural differences."

Self-actualization

The pinnacle of Maslow's hierarcy, self-actualization, is very difficult to achieve; however, according to Professor *A*, Student *B* is very driven and focused, and works incredibly hard at her own self-development. She is strong in her convictions and when she has a dream or a vision, she operationalizes it in daily life and stays true to her goal. Also, to be self-actualized one must first know what he or she wants to be in life, and to date, Student *B* is on track to meeting her educational goals and moving into a career that will be both emotionally satisfying and financially rewarding. Professor *A* attempts to provide the necessary support that Student *B* requires by having lengthy conversations regarding life in general and the incredible opportunities that can be available with an MBA degree. Student B has now graduated with a Bachelor of Commerce degree in Marketing and is currently completing two MBA courses this summer. Her plan is to graduate with her MBA in May 2013.

DISCUSSIONS AND CONCLUSION

The study demonstrates that at least for this particular student and professor, the benefits of a strong mentorship and an extended social support system for a CESL student can serve to facilitate the student's academic learning and cultural acceptance. Each week, Student *B* becomes more familiar with the American culture and gains a better understanding of its quirks and intricacies. At the same time, however, she manages to hold on to her Chinese culture by Skyping her family members and friends and visiting the young Chinese family who live around the corner from Professor *A*'s house.

Professor *A* has also gained incredible insights into the Chinese culture and the needs of CESL students as they seek to acclimate to the North American way of life. This feat was accomplished through numerous conversations in English which also assisted Student *B* with her English language skills and provided Professor *A* with a newfound understanding when advising and grading the academic work of CESL students and other international students whose native language is not English.

While the first year of the two-year longitudinal study provided an environment to gain insight into effectively mentoring CESL students and appreciating an increased sensitivity for cultural understanding, one limitation of the study was that only two people were studied and interviewed. Therefore, a generalization of the results might be limited due to the fact that only one professor and one student were involved. It is suggested that future studies should include more students and professors from different backgrounds, disciplines and institutions. The plan is to conduct further interviews next year and gather information as to how needs can be successfully met in order to facilitate the CESL student's academic goals.

The following is a list of strategies to improve mentoring experience, which were discussed during interviews with Professor *A* and Student *B*. The purpose of the strategies is to improve North American professors' understanding of cultural needs and differences and assist the CESL students in achieving educational excellence and cultural competency.

1.   Accept, respect, and embrace diversity;
2.   Communicate daily (Seek first to understand then be understood (Stephen Covey);
3.   Reflect and then attempt new solutions as necessary;
4.   Mentoring is a two-way process. Remember to be as open to learning as you are to teaching;
5.   The more you give the more you receive;
6.   Be creative- think outside the box;
7.   Celebrate successes;
8.   Take the time to enjoy the experience;
9.   Do unto others as they would do unto themselves;
10. We can learn from our mistakes and turn failure into opportunity.

REFERENCES

Canadian Bureau for International Education. (2002, April 15). *International student numbers hit record high, but Canada offers dwindling support for African students.* Retrieved October 28, 2002 from the World Wide Web:http://www.cbie.ca/news/index_e.cfm?folder=releasesandpage=rel_2002-04-15_e

Cherry, K. (2012). *Maslow's needs hierarchy.* Retrieved on June 29, 2012 from http://psychology.about.com/od/theoriesofpersonality/ss/maslows-needs-hierarchy_4.htm

Duffy, K. (2004). *Failing students: A qualitative study of factors that influence the decisions regarding assessment of students' competence in practice.* Nursing and Midwifery Council, London.

Huang, J. (1998). *Students' learning difficulties in a second language speaking classroom.* Paper presented at the Annual Meeting of the American Educational Research Association, San Diego, CA. (ERIC Document Reproduction Service No. ED 420 193)

Huang, J. (2004). Voices from Chinese students: Professors' use of English affects academic listening. *College Student Journal, 38*(2), 212-223.

Huang, J. (2005). Challenges of academic listening in English: Reports by Chinese students. *College Student Journal, 39*(3), 553-569.

Huang, J. (2006). English abilities for academic listening: How confident are Chinese students? *College Student Journal, 40*(1), 218-226.

Huang, J., and Klinger, D. (2006). Chinese graduate students at North American universities: Learning challenges and coping strategies. *The Canadian and International Education Journal, 35*(2), 48-61.

Institute of International Education. (2001, May 16). *98/99 opendoors on the Web.* [Selections from the book], New York. Retrieved June 15, 2002, from the World Wide Web: http://www.opendoorsweb.org/Lead%20Stories/international_studs.htm

McLeod, S. A. (2012). *Maslow's hierarchy of needs.* Retrieved on June 26, 2012, from http://www.simplypsychology.org/maslow.html

Pritchard, E. (2012). Effective mentoring in the community setting. *British Journal of Community Nursing, 17*(3), 119-124.

INDEX

A

academic achievement, 141, 142

academic anxiety, xiii, xiv, 15, 19, 20, 21, 22, 23, 24, 35, 58, 60, 143

academic difficulties, 138

academic learning, xiii, xiv, xv, xvi, 3, 4, 11, 15, 16, 17, 19, 20, 21, 24, 27, 35, 36, 37, 39, 44, 49, 50, 52, 53, 54, 56, 57, 59, 63, 64, 68, 76, 84, 109, 112, 115, 116, 141, 142, 143, 147

academic lectures, xiv, xv, 9, 17, 22, 27, 28, 32, 33, 51, 52, 68, 70, 80, 95, 96, 99, 104, 108, 110, 112, 113, 116, 117, 118, 119, 120

academic listening, xiv, xv, 13, 25, 27, 28, 29, 31, 32, 33, 34, 44, 45, 61, 72, 75, 76, 80, 81, 91, 95, 96, 98, 99, 104, 105, 107, 108, 109, 112, 113, 114, 120, 121, 123, 138, 148

academic listening skills, 99

academic performance, 19, 22

academic studies, xiii, 3, 4, 12, 16, 18, 28, 36, 49, 57, 63, 64, 66, 83, 84

academic study skills, 4, 12, 27, 36

academic success, xiii, xvi, 22, 107, 108, 141, 142, 143

academic tasks, 19

academic writing, xv, 40

acculturation, xiv, 7, 28, 35, 40, 43, 44, 59, 143

active thinking, 76

activity theory, 46, 50, 61

adaptation, 13, 14, 19, 24, 25, 34, 45, 46, 60, 61, 72, 73, 121, 122

adaptations, 14, 25, 34, 46, 73

administrators, xiii, 4, 16, 36, 64, 83

adolescents, 13

affective factors, xiv, 49, 54, 58, 60

American culture, xiii, 4, 5, 6, 7, 9, 10, 11, 12, 16, 17, 23, 43, 44, 50, 59, 63, 67, 71, 80, 88, 96, 147

American Educational Research Association, 25, 45, 61, 148

ANOVA, 29, 30, 31, 32, 76, 99, 100, 101, 102, 103, 113

anxiety, xiii, xiv, 7, 15, 16, 19, 20, 21, 22, 23, 24, 35, 38, 40, 43, 53, 55, 58, 60, 63, 68, 84, 88, 143

APA, 40

aptitude, 108

Asia, 109

Asian countries, 64

assessment, xiv, xvi, xvii, 72, 125, 126, 127, 128, 129, 131, 137, 138, 139, 140, 148

atmosphere, 6, 11, 37, 59, 67, 88

attitudes, 38, 53, 84

authenticity, 105, 121

authorities, 6, 7, 17, 37, 38, 42, 50, 51, 57, 58, 64, 65, 68, 69, 84, 86, 109, 111, 117

authority, 7, 8, 13, 42, 52, 57, 64, 69, 115

B

basic needs, 142

behaviors, 6, 17, 36, 38, 50, 64, 67, 84, 109, 111

benefits, 8, 73, 140, 142, 145, 147

bicultural conflicts, 7

body language, 104

C

CAP, 128

case study, xvi, 110, 120, 139, 141, 142, 143

challenges, xiii, xiv, xv, xvi, xvii, 3, 4, 8, 9, 11, 12, 13, 16, 18, 19, 21, 22, 23, 25, 27, 28, 33, 35, 36, 38, 39, 40, 41, 42, 43, 44, 50, 52, 58, 61, 63, 64, 66, 68, 69, 71, 72, 73, 75, 80, 84, 85, 88, 89, 91, 95, 96, 97, 99, 100, 101, 103, 104, 107, 108, 109, 110, 112, 113, 118, 119, 120, 139, 140, 143, 148

China, xiii, xvii, 3, 7, 8, 11, 13, 14, 15, 18, 19, 21, 22, 23, 24, 31, 32, 34, 35, 37, 41, 42, 45, 46, 49, 52, 54, 55, 56, 57, 59, 60, 63, 64, 65, 66, 67, 68,

70, 72, 80, 83, 86, 87, 88, 89, 100, 101, 109, 111, 113, 116, 120, 121, 130, 141, 143, 145, 146
Chinese culture, xiii, 6, 7, 11, 16, 17, 37, 42, 43, 51, 52, 57, 58, 64, 65, 66, 68, 69, 86, 88, 111, 115, 147
class size, 69, 117
classes, 9, 42, 43, 58, 60, 69, 89, 90, 101, 104, 108, 110, 116, 117, 118, 120, 122, 146
classroom, xiv, xv, 3, 5, 6, 8, 9, 10, 11, 12, 13, 14, 16, 17, 18, 21, 23, 24, 25, 35, 38, 40, 41, 42, 44, 45, 51, 53, 56, 57, 60, 61, 63, 68, 69, 71, 72, 80, 81, 83, 84, 85, 86, 87, 88, 89, 90, 91, 96, 97, 98, 104, 107, 110, 111, 113, 117, 119, 121, 143, 148
classroom culture, 23, 84, 117
classroom environment, xv, 42, 83, 89, 90
classroom instruction, xv, 16, 18, 84, 107, 119
classroom learning environment, xiv, 35, 40, 41, 44, 88, 90, 143
classroom learning strategy, 81
classroom settings, 38
cognitive factors, xiv, 49, 54, 60
college students, 12, 24, 33, 45, 60, 71, 121
colleges, 22, 66
colloquial language, 97, 98
communication, xiii, 7, 10, 13, 16, 17, 25, 34, 37, 46, 52, 56, 61, 64, 73, 108, 126, 129
communication gap, 126
communication skills, 10, 129
communication styles, xiii, 16, 64
communities, 10, 60
community, 9, 11, 66, 142, 145, 148
community participation, 43
competitiveness, 7, 65
comprehension, xv, 9, 12, 34, 38, 69, 70, 71, 75, 76, 77, 78, 79, 80, 81, 85, 89, 98, 99, 100, 101, 102, 103, 105, 108, 109, 110, 113, 114, 115, 116, 117, 119, 120, 121, 122, 123
confidence levels, xiii
confrontation, 14, 25, 46, 61, 73, 91, 121
Confucian philosophy, 6, 17, 36, 50, 64, 65, 66, 84
Confucianism, xv, 63
Confucian-oriented learning, 17, 36, 84, 109
Confucian-Socratic framework, 16, 36, 84, 85, 90, 109
Confucius, 6, 7, 12, 16, 17, 24, 36, 37, 45, 50, 60, 64, 65, 66, 71, 73, 84, 90, 109
construct validity, 139
constructivism, xv, 63
constructivist learning, 46, 61
conversations, 7, 8, 10, 143, 146, 147
coping strategies, xiii, xiv, xvi, xvii, 13, 25, 35, 36, 38, 39, 40, 44, 45, 61, 72, 91, 139, 148
course work, 126

creative thinking, 57
critical thinking, xiv, 18, 35, 40, 42, 44, 58, 60, 87, 89, 143
critical thinking skills, xiv, 35, 40, 42, 44, 143
cross-cultural class, 85, 90
cross-cultural learning, xvi, 24, 39, 42, 45, 50, 59, 60, 85, 139
cross-cultural learning issues, xvi
cultural background, xiii, xvi, 6, 16, 56, 80, 83
cultural capital, 10
cultural context, 9, 10, 14, 16, 25, 36, 46, 61, 73, 84, 85, 91, 109, 116, 120, 121
cultural differences, xiii, xiv, xv, 11, 15, 16, 21, 22, 44, 54, 64, 66, 68, 142, 146
cultural environment, 4, 36, 49, 50, 64, 66, 95, 107, 108, 126
cultural facilitator, 143
cultural factors, 4, 12, 24, 50, 63, 64
cultural shock, 39, 57, 89
cultural studies, xiv, 3, 4
cultural values, 37, 42, 66
culture, xiii, xiv, 3, 6, 7, 9, 10, 11, 12, 13, 14, 16, 17, 21, 23, 24, 27, 34, 36, 37, 42, 43, 49, 50, 51, 52, 57, 58, 59, 64, 65, 66, 67, 68, 69, 71, 72, 80, 84, 86, 88, 89, 111, 115, 117, 119, 121, 142, 147
culture alignments, 10

D

deep learners, xiv, 3, 5
deep understanding, 5
depression, 7
discourse markers, xv, 12, 71, 95, 97, 99, 103, 104, 105, 108, 120
discrimination, 7

E

education, xiii, xiv, xvi, 4, 7, 13, 15, 17, 22, 23, 24, 36, 50, 56, 57, 59, 60, 64, 65, 66, 73, 84, 109, 127, 130, 139
educational assessment, 130
educational background, 49, 64, 142
educational culture, 27, 36, 49, 142
educational experience, 9, 44, 56, 59
educational factors, xiv, 49, 54
educational research, 59
educational system, xiii, 4, 9, 16, 36, 49, 50, 59, 64, 66, 95, 107, 108, 126
educators, xiii, 4, 5, 12, 16, 24, 36, 64, 77, 83, 109, 130
emotional challenges, xiii, 16, 18, 19

empirical studies, xiv, 126, 127, 128
employment, xiv, 15, 22, 41, 55, 59
England, 14, 41, 56, 105
English abilities, xiv, 13, 21, 25, 27, 28, 29, 32, 33, 61, 72, 148
English language, 40
English language proficiency, 28, 40, 49, 52, 57, 76, 77, 80, 142
English language skills, xv, 75, 147
English proficiency, xiii, 4, 12, 16, 17, 19, 21, 27, 28, 29, 36, 37, 40, 57, 60, 63, 99, 126
English-speaking environment, 22
environment, 4, 6, 7, 12, 17, 22, 31, 33, 36, 37, 41, 44, 49, 50, 55, 64, 66, 71, 81, 89, 95, 107, 108, 143, 147
environmental adaptation, 19
environments, 46, 61, 68, 119, 126
equality, 7, 38, 51, 68, 84, 87, 111
equity, 137
ESL writing assessments, 126
Europe, 41, 56
examinations, 58, 65, 66, 128
exercise, 144
expertise, xvii, 9
exposure, 22, 84
extended social support system, xvi, 141, 143, 147

F

facilitators of learning, 17, 38, 51, 69, 86, 117
fairness, xvii, 126, 136, 137
financial burdens, 16, 18, 21
financial concerns, 7
financial difficulties, xiii, xiv, 15, 16, 17, 19, 22, 27, 35, 36, 37, 39, 40, 44, 63, 143
financial factors, xiv, 49, 50, 54
financial problems, 52, 60
financial support, 18, 40, 44, 52, 58, 59, 60

G

generalizability, xvii, 125, 126, 127, 128, 129, 130, 138, 139, 140
Generalizability (*G*-) coefficient ix, xvi, 125, 132, 134, 135, 136
Generalizability (*G*-) theory, xv, 125
graduate students, xiii, xiv, xv, 3, 13, 15, 16, 17, 18, 19, 20, 23, 24, 25, 28, 30, 31, 32, 33, 35, 36, 37, 39, 40, 41, 42, 43, 44, 45, 46, 49, 50, 51, 52, 53, 54, 55, 57, 58, 59, 60, 61, 64, 71, 72, 73, 76, 78, 83, 84, 85, 88, 89, 90, 91, 99, 100, 101, 102, 103, 112, 114, 115, 116, 125, 126, 127, 129, 130, 136, 137, 139, 142, 148

H

hidden inequalities, 5
hierarchy of needs, xvi, 141, 142, 143, 148
higher education, 65, 72, 126, 130
higher-level thinking skills, 38
Hong Kong, 14

I

identity, xiv, 3, 4, 5, 6, 8, 13, 14
inactive learners, 6
inclusive mentoring process, 142
independent variable, 29, 31, 76, 78, 101, 113, 115, 116, 117
individual development, 46, 61, 65
individualism, 7
individuals, 17, 3
inequality, 8
in-group memberships, 9, 10, 12
institutions, xvi, 40, 109, 125, 126, 147
instructional factors, xv, 68, 70, 84, 85, 107, 114, 119
instructional styles, 17, 38, 51
instructional tasks, 96
interaction effects, 132
interactional listening, 108
interactive discourse, 96, 110
intercultural adjustment, 17, 52
intercultural experience, 141, 142
intervention, 13, 24
intonation, 98
invisible biases, 5
IRT, xvii
item response theory, xvii

L

L1, 57, 81, 138
L2, 57, 81, 96, 138, 140
language abilities, 28, 32, 79
language barrier, xiv, 7, 15, 21, 22, 23
language components, 29, 32, 79
language proficiency, 28, 40, 49, 52, 57, 76, 77, 80, 81, 142
language skills, xv, 23, 71, 75, 147
languages, 98, 119, 132, 133, 140
Latin America, 109

learners, xiv, 3, 5, 6, 19, 38, 57, 76, 97, 98, 108, 109, 110
learning activity, 50
learning approaches, xiii, xiv, xvi, 3, 5, 57
learning challenges, xiii, xvi, xvii, 13, 25, 36, 38, 39, 44, 61, 72, 91, 139, 148
learning culture, 57
learning difficulties, 23, 45, 61, 64, 148
learning disabilities, 25
learning efficiency, 19
learning environment, xiv, 6, 12, 17, 35, 37, 40, 41, 44, 46, 61, 71, 88, 90, 143
learning outcomes, xvii
learning process, xvi, 8, 11, 18, 19, 45, 80, 141
learning skills, 76, 80
learning strategies, xv, 9, 42, 83, 85, 86, 89, 90, 110, 118
learning styles, xiii, 16, 64
lecture comprehension, xv, 38, 69, 70, 75, 76, 77, 78, 79, 80, 81, 85, 100, 101, 102, 103, 105, 108, 109, 110, 114, 115, 116, 117, 119, 121, 122, 123
lecture discourse, 96, 97, 105, 110
lecture organization, xv, 8, 52, 70, 85, 107, 114, 119
lecture summary, xv, 8, 70, 107, 114, 116, 119, 122
legal frustrations, 16, 40, 41
legal issues, 41
legal status, 18, 55, 59
Likert scale, 29, 76, 99, 107, 112
linear modeling, xvii
linguistic challenges, 33, 99, 104, 112
linguistic factors, xiv, 49, 54, 99, 113
lipid peroxidation, 72
listening skills, 79, 80, 105, 109, 121
listening tasks, 96, 108
literacy, 12
love and belongingness needs, 142

M

macromarkers, 97
Mandarin, 28, 105
materials, 42, 57, 65, 71, 87, 89, 118, 121
mathematics, xiv, 15, 20, 21, 23, 56, 104, 119
measurement, 128, 133, 134, 135, 138
membrane permeability, 72
memorization, 5, 42, 58, 60, 89
memorizing, 58
memory, xv, 75, 76, 77, 78, 80, 81
mental health, 10
mentor, 7, 38, 84, 86, 111, 142, 144
mentoring program, 142, 143, 144
mentorship, 142, 144, 147

methodology, 6, 8, 34, 38, 44, 53, 73, 81, 84, 113, 119, 121, 128
micro-level discourse markers, 96, 110
mode of teaching, 7, 8
mother tongue, 57, 126
multicultural education, 24, 71
multiculturalism, 45

N

non-linguistic factors, 99, 113
non-verbal cues, 96
North American culture, xiii, 4, 5, 6, 7, 9, 10, 11, 12, 16, 17, 21, 23, 37, 43, 44, 50, 63, 67, 71
North American professors, xiii, xiv, xv, xvi, 8, 9, 17, 23, 24, 44, 50, 60, 63, 64, 84, 90, 99, 147
North American universities, xiii, xiv, xv, xvi, 3, 4, 5, 6, 7, 10, 11, 13, 15, 16, 17, 18, 19, 20, 21, 22, 23, 24, 25, 27, 28, 35, 36, 37, 38, 39, 40, 43, 44, 45, 49, 50, 52, 53, 54, 57, 59, 60, 61, 63, 64, 65, 66, 67, 68, 72, 83, 84, 85, 86, 90, 91, 125, 139, 141, 142, 148

O

oral presentations, 22, 40, 88, 89
othering, 6
otherness, 8, 10
others, 4, 6, 10, 11, 17, 18, 36, 55, 84, 98, 109, 147
outside-classroom communities, 10

P

passive learners, xiv, 3, 5, 38
peer rejection, 10
peer support, 42
physiological needs, 142, 144
pragmatic learning, 6, 7, 17, 37, 50, 65, 84, 109
pragmatism, 42
pronunciation, xv, 29, 30, 33, 79, 95, 99, 101, 104, 110
prosodic features, 97, 98
public policy, 138

Q

qualitative differences, 14
query, xv, 63
questioning, 17, 36, 38, 84, 85, 109, 119

R

Rasch analysis, 128
Rasch measurement, 138, 139, 140
rater variability, xvi, 125, 127, 128
rating consistency, 126, 127
rating scale, 140
reading, xiv, 5, 11, 18, 27, 29, 31, 32, 38, 40, 42, 44, 52, 67, 70, 78, 79, 88, 89, 107, 108, 116, 118, 120, 126, 145
reading comprehension, 32
reform, 6, 7, 16, 17, 36, 50, 65, 84, 109

S

safety needs, 142, 145
scholarship, 18, 21, 22, 59, 146
score reliability, 128, 129, 138
score variability, 128, 130, 131
score variation, xv, 125, 130, 134, 135
second language, 13, 25, 34, 45, 46, 60, 61, 73, 81, 105, 121, 126, 127, 128, 129, 138, 140, 148
security, 44, 142, 145
self-actualization, xvi, 141, 142, 144, 146
self-centeredness, 38, 68, 111
self-confidence, xiv, 15, 22, 68
self-efficacy, 63
self-esteem, xvi, 10, 141, 142, 144, 146
self-expression, xiii, 16, 64
self-report data, 29, 33, 70, 85, 120
self-study, 89, 115
semi-structured interviews, 39, 53, 85
short-term memory, xv, 75, 76, 77, 78, 80
social activities, 10, 17, 18, 19, 23, 37, 43, 52, 57, 59, 66
social communication skills, 10
social communicative competence, xiv, 3
Social communicative competence, 10
social communicative effectiveness, 10
social environment, 10
social identities, 4
social integration, 13
social interactions, 10
social isolation, 10
social life, xiv, 10, 15, 22
social maladjustment, 10
social relationships, 65
social sciences, 17, 18, 23, 46, 55, 61, 127
social skills, 143
social status, 65
social support, xiv, xvi, 141, 142, 143, 147
societal harmony, 7, 17, 36, 50, 65, 84, 109

society, xiii, 6, 11, 14, 36, 59, 64, 66, 67, 88
socio-cultural factors, xiv, 49, 54, 59
Socrates, 17, 36, 84, 109
Socratic-oriented learning, 17, 36, 84, 109
speech, xv, 41, 55, 95, 96, 97, 98, 99, 100, 101, 104
speech acts, 96
spending, 42, 44
spirit of equality, 7, 38, 51, 68, 84, 87, 111
state anxiety, 19, 24
stress, 38, 43, 51, 53, 65, 68, 69, 71, 73, 84, 86, 87, 98, 117
stressors, 12, 24, 33, 45, 60, 71, 121
structural equation modeling, xvii, 129, 140
structure, 38, 50, 53, 57, 76, 97, 108, 110, 130, 135, 137
structuring, 8, 69, 110
student's expectations, xv, 83, 86, 87, 90
student's role, xv, 83, 86, 87, 90
study skills, 4, 12, 23, 27, 36, 49, 63, 105, 120, 142
surface learners, xiv, 3

T

teacher training, 45
teachers, 6, 7, 8, 9, 14, 17, 18, 38, 41, 42, 50, 51, 53, 57, 58, 64, 65, 66, 67, 68, 69, 70, 71, 84, 85, 86, 87, 88, 98, 100, 101, 102, 103, 104, 111, 113, 114, 115, 116, 117, 118, 119, 120, 122, 123, 128
teaching experience, 21, 127
test anxiety, 22
Test of English as a Foreign Language, 17, 28, 52, 76, 129
test scores, 127, 139
testing, 127, 138, 140
think critically, 87, 89
TOEFL, 17, 27, 28, 29, 40, 52, 57, 76, 105, 112, 121, 122, 129, 139
trademarks, 17
traditions, 11, 67, 68, 111
training, 9, 127, 136, 140
trait anxiety, 19, 24
transactional listening, 108

U

undergraduate education, 3, 16, 35, 56, 64, 65, 83
universities, xiii, xiv, xv, xvi, xvii, 3, 4, 5, 6, 7, 10, 11, 13, 14, 15, 16, 17, 18, 19, 20, 21, 22, 23, 24, 25, 27, 28, 31, 33, 35, 36, 37, 38, 39, 40, 43, 44, 45, 46, 49, 50, 52, 53, 54, 56, 57, 58, 59, 60, 61, 63, 64, 65, 66, 67, 68, 70, 72, 73, 75, 76, 80, 83,

84, 85, 86, 90, 91, 95, 107, 108, 109, 111, 112, 116, 120, 121, 125, 139, 141, 142, 148

V

validity of the assessment, xvi, 125
variables, 29, 76, 99, 113, 117
vocabulary, 29, 31, 33, 79, 80, 101, 102, 104

W

Washington, 13, 71
Western educators, 5
Western instructors, 5
writing process, 40
writing tasks, xv, 127, 129